FOUNDER'S OFFICE

SARTHAK AHUJA

wyzr

Published by Wyzr Content Pvt. Ltd.

ISBN (Hardcover): 978-81-962223-6-9
ISBN (Paperback): 978-81-962223-5-2
ISBN (eBook): 978-81-962223-4-5

Editors: Amlan Chakravarty, Vinit Aggarwal, Yashraj Sharma

Typeset in Adobe InDesign by Kajal Ahuja

Cover by Syed Rizvi

Printed and bound by Manipal Technologies Limited

First printing edition 2023

Also by the same author:

Daily Coffee & Startup Fundraising
A comprehensive guide to starting up in India

Contents

Part 2
Business Finance: Measure What Matters

Part 3
Sales & Marketing: Let Them Know, Make Them Buy

Part 4
Startup Notes: Things Startups Go Through

Part 5
Fundraising: Getting Money in the Bank

Introduction

In very basic terms, what separates a great business leader from the average, is their ability to take the right decisions at a higher frequency. The results of these decisions come out at least a few weeks (often, years) after they were taken. What's common about all decisions is that no one can claim with absolute certainty if they are right or wrong. Only the results tell us which were right and you must wait for them.

Since the outcome can't be predicted with certainty, these leaders use the information at hand, their past experience of dealing with problems, and their judgement for decision-making. But not everyone can experience all business problems on their own, and to be effective, they should also learn from others' experiences and have processes in place to minimize risk and maximize output.

This book has been written to equip leaders at any level - an entire organization, a region, a branch, an office, or even a small team - with information that can help them make better decisions.

It's a collection of 150+ impactful lessons I've collated over the 11 years of working with organizations of different sizes and through an extensive study on business in general. It's unusual in the sense that the chapters, although categorized accurately, don't follow a strict order. The idea was to give actionable business insights on every page without diluting the impact. If you read it in the given order, great! If you don't and just open any page randomly, you still find something immediately useful without the baggage of context. But if you're used to reading books with well-structured narratives, you'd need to recalibrate your expectations here. This is more a deck of cards with each card containing a useful note, rather than one long book.

My recommendation - check the parts in which the book has been divided, start with the one you need the most help on, and then move to others as you deem fit. My hope is that it serves you the same way your revision notes did before you took an exam. The good thing here is that the exam is an open-book one. The not-so-good thing is that it's perpetual. It just never ends. So this book should be an able constant companion in your professional journey.

Lastly, I assess myself on the value I add to anyone who associates with me. By picking up this book, you have shown your faith in me, and I'm truly grateful for that. I'd love your feedback on whether the book delivers the intended value or not, be it on social DMs or on Amazon, Goodreads, or Wyzr.

And if you indeed find it valuable, do *share it with someone who may need it!*

Part 1
Leadership:
Taking the Right Decisions

The first section of the book covers general business concepts and frameworks. You may have come across some of them yourself - Porter's 5 Forces, the concept of moat, red ocean vs. blue ocean, and more. And there would be others which you may not have seen earlier - like a framework for luck, or calculating the number of freeloaders in your company.

Broadly, the goal of this section is to provide food for thought to any entrepreneur, leader, or manager, give them new perspectives, and help them build better strategic muscle.

In all chapters, I've summarized these concepts in a way I believe is simple to understand, with actionable advice at the end.

Like with everything else in the book, there's no strict order to follow. One page at a time, one lesson at a time.

1. First Who, Then What

What do you think is the most important factor that determines business success? Is it market size? The product? Or something else?

Steve Jobs once explained in an interview - "If you do the right things on the top line, the bottom line will follow." He elaborated upon it by saying that if you have the right strategy, the right people, and the right culture, you'll anyway get your product, marketing, and operations right, and that will take care of the bottom line.

Even data has shown that what matters much more than market size, industry, tech advancement and product quality for a business's success is the cultural and value fit among the founding team members.

Jim Collins, author of *Good to Great* and other successful business books, has mentioned time and again: "First Who, Then What".

And what has shown to matter much more than technical skills are matters of value - integrity, character, and ambition. All of them have to be similar in the founding team for them to survive every phase of disruption and value creation in a changing environment, where new technical skills will keep getting acquired by the team members over time.

The co-founders must have the same ambition, but not the same aspiration. This has also been explained very well by the TaxiForSure founder, Raghunandan G, through the context that both founders may want success for the business, but one may get more media attention and the other may not necessarily have the same aspiration, which helps.

Remember - First Who, Then What.

2. Identifying Latent Needs

Do you know what happens when you skip a song within 30 seconds on Spotify?

Google built its entire business on the back of search. Amazon has probably the highest search traffic in the world. People these days search brands and products first on Instagram and Amazon before they do so on Google.

But what keeps a tech business - be it Amazon, Instagram, Google, Netflix or even Spotify ahead of its competition is not the search feature, but the *recommendation* algorithm.

You solve a customer pain point by recommending something to the user that they may want, even though they consciously don't even know it.

This is called cracking the problem of identifying a consumer's latent need (something they don't know themselves), and serving it on a plate to them so that they are:

1. Delighted

2. More engaged with your platform

3. Prompted to spend money

For example, if you skip a song on Spotify in under 30 seconds, it understands you don't like it and the recommendation algorithm will most likely not show it to you again.

As a small business or startup, if you can collect data and build a solution not for an existing consumer problem, but serve something that the consumer did not even know they wanted - you have the potential to make much more money.

3. Red Ocean vs Blue Ocean

The terms "Red Ocean" and "Blue Ocean" were first coined by Chan Kim & Renée Mauborgne to denote types of markets - red being known markets with existing products and services - and a number of competitors fighting with each other to get a limited set of customers. The fighting between suppliers turns the ocean red, which is a zero-sum game. The size of the pie for the taking is limited.

Blue Ocean is a new market providing a product or a service that caters to a latent need, so far not identified as a problem, or a feasible solution - which makes your business a unique solution provider - in a deep blue ocean.

Examples of Blue Oceans:

› Apple's iPod created a new category of product different from a CD player

› Uber transformed the way the cab industry operates

› Airbnb built a hotel stay business without owning any hotels

Blue Oceans:

› Create new demands that did not earlier exist

› Make the competition irrelevant

› Help the company build a strategy that is both differentiated and low cost

To build a business in a Blue Ocean, one has to:

› Identify new trends of demand creation or consumer behaviour

› Study new technologies that are available, and how they can be applied to disrupt existing solutions

4. What's Your Moat?

When I sometimes ask startup founders, "What's your moat?", I've often seen puzzled looks. Once someone even asked me the full form for the word, probably associating with G.O.A.T.

Well, "moat" is the competitive advantage that your business/product has over the competition. It's derived from the trench that would surround a castle and protect it from invaders.

It's what protects you from competition, makes you defensible in the market, and does not have a full form.

I saw an illustration on Greg Isenberg's Twitter that beautifully explained the 6 types of moats.

1. "Brand", which he calls "better marketing" - Nike is the best example, yeah?

2. "Quality", an attribute that everyone uses to justify why their product is higher priced than the competition. You could say JBL, or Bang & Olufsen, of course, as Greg does.

3. "Price" - that's competing at scale for the masses. Think BoAt in the context of audio equipment/wearables.

4. "Community", or the audience/fandom you've built around your product. I'd say look at all your cohort-based courses or even the MBA programs. The learning

from peers and the alum network is priceless.

5. "Technology", which is your patents and designs and copyrights and all intellectual property that you have legal rights to use commercially till China copies your Apple watch Ultra and starts selling it at Rs 3k.
6. And "Network Effects" - that's probably no longer Uber/Ola, but definitely WhatsApp.

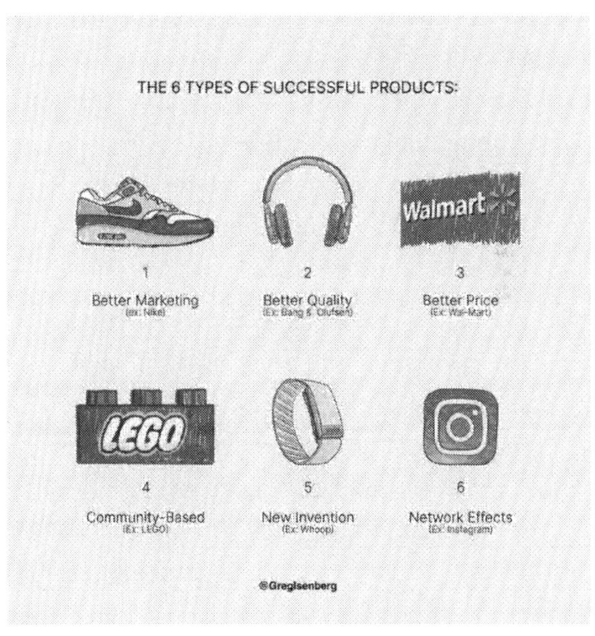

5. ABC of Tech

There are two types of business problems that you can solve through your startup idea.

Type 1: Doing old things more efficiently - faster, cheaper, more convenient.

Type 2: Doing new things that were not possible earlier.

Most founders focus on Type 1 problems because they are easy to observe. And because they are easy to observe, they attract more competition.

Type 2 problems, when solved, create a far greater impact in the world through the pathbreaking use of new technology for an unimagined use case. This comes with studying new technologies in-depth with an understanding of how they could solve existing problems.

For example, using blockchain technology not just for decentralized payments, but thinking about how that can fix logistics issues for say, Tier 2 India; or how can it build a system to consolidate communication modes such as email, WhatsApp, voice notes, all in one. Can it?

Interestingly, Marc Andreesen of a16z stated in 2022 that there would three areas of study that will bring the next revolution in business ideas. He called it the ABC of Tech.

A › Artificial Intelligence: GPT-4, DALL-E, OpenAI

B › BioTech: Genomics, mRNA, combining biology with

engineering

C › Crypto: Distributed Consensus, Distributed Trust Networks

The first one has certainly materialized.

6. Financial Objective of Any Business

A business's financial objective is NOT to make a PROFIT.

This is not just in the context of startups, but also for family businesses/ MSMEs.

The financial objective of a business is actually to manage POSITIVE CASH FLOWS.

It's best to get positive cash flows from operating activities i.e. selling products, services, subscriptions, etc.

But till the time the operating activities don't turn positive cash flows, the purpose is managed through financing activities of raising debt or equity from external investors.

This slight change in the perspective of the financial objective of a business from profit to cash flows helps people appreciate the fact that a business can be loss-making in the first few years if it is continuing to generate positive cash flows. Real discipline lies in knowing that the time till when one can use financing activities to manage positive cash flows instead of operating cash flows should be limited—and not overstretched.

As an example, it may be reasonable for a startup to raise external capital and use it for:

- Building a good product or bearing a high capital expenditure for set up

- Launch and marketing spend
- Collecting consumer insights and feedback
- Improving the product and spend on making it habit forming

But how much time would you allow a business to do this through external funds till it turns profitable?

I believe in most cases, it should not stretch beyond 5-7 years. There are exceptions, but then it's a function of the risk appetite of the investors.

Stretch it beyond 7 years of you not being able to generate positive "cash flows from operations", and sustainability can get difficult.

Soon, the focus will change from creating value for consumers to being forced to create value for investors at the cost of consumers or incoming retail investors.

Now, let's look at it in the context of MSMEs.

MSMEs make money but don't show high profits to reduce tax liability. There are enough ways to plan taxes legitimately, and legally, if one knows how to manage cash flows. One can borrow capital, invest in fixed assets, charge depreciation and interest to cash flows and do a hundred other things to save tax.

So even when you see a family-owned / MSME business financials, don't judge them by their profits. There is a lot they've probably done at the end of the cash flow.

Because "profit" is an opinion and "cash flow" is the reality.

Good for you to know this mantra if you don't already.

Revenues are Vanity.

Profits are Sanity.

Cash flow is the Reality.

7. Vision or Data?

Most people don't realise what the iPod was originally built for.

Its purpose wasn't just to play music, but to sell Macintosh computers.

That's what was in Steve Jobs' head: "We're going to make something amazing that will only work with our Macs. People will love it so much that they will start buying Macs again."

At that time, Apple had almost no market share. Not even in the US. But the iPod would solve that problem and save the company.

So as far as Steve Jobs was concerned, the iPod would never work with a Windows PC. And that's why the first generation of the iPod fizzled.

The critics as well as existing Apple users loved it, but there were barely any to begin with.

The iPod cost $399 and the iMac cost $1300. But no one was going to spend $1700 dollars on the package just to listen to crisper sound on Linkin Park songs.

The team went to Steve, asking him to allow for the second version to work with Windows computers, but he wouldn't budge from his vision.

The team toiled months to convince him that in this battle, data had to come first, consumer insight second, and vision third.

They agreed on letting Walt Mossberg, a famous tech reviewer, cast the deciding vote and the second-generation iPod allowed Windows PC owners to transfer music to the device.

This changed the trajectory for Apple immediately and sales skyrocketed to tens of millions annually.

This also led people to love Apple so much that they started switching over to Apple's other products - and sales for the Mac started rising again.

The moral of the story is that you'll have both data on consumer insights and vision to take a business decision.

Vision works when there is no data, and once you start capturing data on consumer insights, that has to take precedence over vision for decisions, with Vision being a long-term over-arching guiding force.

8. Framework for SWOT Analysis

Most founders miss this while doing a SWOT analysis of their business idea.

It's so surprising to see that the easiest and the most important tool for business SWOT analysis is taught in 11th Standard Business Studies, but is forgotten or disregarded by most founders while evaluating their own business idea.

It's the Porter's 5 Forces Model popularised by the Harvard Business School professor Michael Porter, and it explains the 5 forces a business needs to tackle well to develop a sustainable moat.

1. **Industry Rivalry:** Larger the number of competitors vying for market share, lesser the power of the company. Prefer to enter a market where you can attempt to be a monopoly or a part of a duopoly.
2. **Threat of New Entrants:** If anyone can easily enter the industry to provide the same product or service, you may not have a sustained advantage to keep making money over a period of time.
3. **Bargaining Power of Suppliers:** If you're dependent on just a few suppliers in the industry, you may not have the power to control costs. And if your suppliers start favouring your competitors over you, it'll be tough to survive.

4. **Bargaining Power of Buyers:** If your business is dependent on just a handful of customers, the risk to your revenue is high if any of them switches to another vendor. More and diversified customer base may mean lower volatility in revenue expectations.

5. **Threat of Substitutes:** Businesses that produce goods or services for which there are close substitutes, may also have to struggle to constantly find ways to differentiate themselves to charge a premium.

Use the above as a framework for carrying out the SWOT(Strengths, Weaknesses, Opportunities, Threats) analysis and while thinking through your moat.

9. Utilize Opportunities

This story has taught me one of the biggest lessons about business.

There was a business competition for a batch of students in a school, where each group was given a capital fund of just Rs 50, using which they had 3 hours to build a business.

The teams would then get 20 mins each to present their business plans, and the one with the largest profit would be declared the winner.

Students ran about. Someone bought chocolates for Rs 50 to sell, another bought stationery… and so on.

When the time for presentations came, the team that trumped most was the one that realized that the Rs 50 worth of capital was just a distraction. They set up a Buy Now Pay Later (BNPL) stall and booked pre-orders for exam notes.

But the team that won realised that even the 3 hours given to build the business was a distraction. They sold their 20-minute presentation slot to an EdTech company for the highest profit, and the company presented their offerings to the entire batch.

I can think of several business lessons from this story:

› We tend to obsess so much on the *constraints* in our business (capital, time, resources) that it takes away our focus from the *opportunities.*

- Leveraging credit and trust helps us make more money, and this is exactly how financial systems and markets work, as we learnt from the BNPL team.
- Intangible assets tend to make bigger returns on the investment than tangible assets.
- B2B business may have higher Average Order Values and margin opportunitie, and also higher willingness to pay than B2C businesses
- Distribution or access to custoemr is a valuable asset that can help you earn a margin from other businesses catering to the same target group (TG).

10. Using Luck Optimally

Here's a way to know which business is luckier than its competitor.

It's from a framework I read about in the book *Great By Choice*, by Jim Collins and Morten T. Hansen.

The book explores the question of why some companies thrive in uncertain and chaotic environments while most falter. The book is based on a nine-year research project that examines companies which achieved exceptional performance during turbulent times. It explains key principles which made these companies successful. One of the key framworks I came across in the book was that of Luck.

Luck is the event which passes each of the following three tests:

1. You did not cause it and had no control over it happening.
2. It has a potentially significant consequence—good or bad.
3. It came as a surprise—be it the timing, the form, or anything.

You look at the history of the company and find events that pass all of these three tests - and mark those events as 'Luck Events'. If the company is the best in its industry, you have to check if they have more luck events in comparison to its competition.

You'll see that most comparable companies have the same number of luck events - but what differentiates the winners is how they managed the event to maximize their *Return on Luck.*

History has shown enough examples of two equally big and qualified companies facing the same luck event, but one squandering it and the other maximising it to increase the Return on Luck.

Also, know that no amount of pure Good Luck will make you Great, but a stroke of Bad Luck can surely kill you. So avoid getting killed by Bad Luck and try to survive through them.

11. 4 Types of Luck

There are 4 types of Luck:

1. Blind Luck
2. Hustle Luck
3. Awareness Luck
4. Expert Luck

- Blind Luck is uncontrollable and what you're born with. The family, environment, geography and resources you're born into. This impacts your early years immensely, till about the late teens and early adulthood.
- Hustle Luck is the one you create by motion and energy that you inject in your ecosystem with your actions to create new opportunities. This defines the 20s for you.
- Awareness Luck is the depth of understanding you have of a particular area or field, which helps you identify early opportunities that you should work towards and create leverage. This sets in when you build experience and awareness in your 30s.
- Expert Luck is the luck you have by knowing about a particular subject in depth and your ability to monetize it because of the opportunities that come your way. This used to be guarded by degrees and credentials, but

even without them, you can build them on the internet by writing, thought leadership and demonstrating your knowledge. This is unique and not related to age in today's time as everyone who wants to learn and has an internet connection can do this today.

While you can't control Type 1, Type 2 and 3 will come with time, and Type 4 is timeless.

This is a version of the Luck Framework by Naval Ravikant, and I think it applies wonderfully to anyone trying to create a business or enterprise of value today.

12. Marchetti Constant

People live within 30 mins of their work. This is the Marchetti Constant.

For millennia, most cities were limited in size because people moved by foot. Even big cities like Ancient Rome or Medieval Paris didn't grow beyond 3 km in diameter. Since people walk at a speed of about 5 km/h, and they are only willing to walk up to 30 min to commute, they were only willing to walk for ~3 km.

Transportation technology has been the biggest factor in determining the size of cities. Whichever city adopted bicycles, grew larger. Same with trams, cars and internal railways.

While horizontal growth was brought in by transportation, vertical growth was brought in by elevators. "*Neeche dukaan, upar makaan*" is not just in Indian culture. It had been all over Europe too.

The same phenomenon applies to businesses. However, here, it's clear, fast, and untarnished "communication" that speeds growth instead of transportation technologies. Most problems in business while scaling up pertain to how well employees, managers, and all departments communicate with each other to achieve the same goal without any misunderstandings.

I feel there can be two macro changes as the first steps to

achieve this.

1. The main objective of Human Resources should be to achieve a culture of clear communication amongst teams with no miscommunications. Their KPIs should be formed in a way to measure this over a period of time. Difficult to measure, but this is where an organization's moat will lie. Reduce miscommunication at all costs; and hire and train people on this extensively.
2. Marketing departments need to develop an "Internal Marketing" function because more than ideas being marketed to the world, they first need to be marketed, accepted, imbibed, and lived in-house. A lot of companies also call this "Corporate Communications".

13. Goldfish, Tech and Longevity

What's the similarity between Goldfish and Tech Companies?

If you take two groups of identical baby fish, put one in abnormally cold water and the other in abnormally warm water, the fish living in cold water grow slower than normal, while those in warm water grow faster.

When you put both groups back in regular-temperature water, they'll eventually converge to become normal, full-sized adults.

Then something interesting happens!

Fish with slowed-down growth in their early days go on to live 30% longer than average. Those with artificial super-charged growth early on die 15% earlier than average.

As Morgan Housel explains this as a lesson to the story on his blog Collab Fund, "Super-charged growth can cause permanent tissue damage and may only be achieved by diversion of resources away from maintenance and repair of damaged biomolecules. Slowed-down growth does the opposite, allowing an increased allocation to maintenance and repair."

The same thing has been found in humans, in birds, in rats... and in Business.

Regardless of the speed at which a business expands, it can be dismantled in half the timespan it needed to grow.

Numerous companies, who once enjoyed the benefits of abundant funds, are currently experiencing this harsh reality. Every business, regardless of the industry, has a natural growth rate, and if you push beyond it, short-term growth comes at the cost of quality and possibly survival.

14. Luxury Is Slow

How many seconds does it take to open an iPhone box? I checked this personally and it took me 4 seconds. This was almost half the time I was promised by a friend, who was sure it takes 7 seconds.

There can be a personal bias in this anecdote, as I've opened the case way too many times and I know my way around the box and the packaging. But in the age of fast-paced activities, Apple designs your unboxing experience to be slow.

While most experts will tell you that it's "anticipation marketing", I feel there's something else at play too.

A simple Google search for "luxury ads" will get you ads made for Rolls Royce, Gucci, etc.

While a BMW ad may emphasize how its car zooms, RR shows even a car chase in slow-motion. If you analyze the ads for Gucci, Versace, or even Balenciaga, what do you see?

Luxury is never fast-paced, it's slow. Wealth brings you the confidence to never be rushed, as it gives you control over time. The key idea that they portray is this, You've made enough wealth to not rush through anything, not even airplanes because private jets wait for you.

So, if you're designing a brand for a product which focuses on the elite, or at least attempts to show itself as one that does, keep it slow.

15. A Framework for Luxury

I've always been intrigued by how luxury brands work and as a result, have been trying to build an exhaustive framework on what makes a brand "luxurious".

On studying brands like Rolls Royce, Patek Phillipe, Rolex, Birkin, Cartier, etc. here are a few things I found.

Firstly, you measure how successful you are as a luxury brand with the following ratio:

"Number of people who know about the brand / Number of people who own the brand" is higher than the competitors by a margin of 100X. The higher the ratio, the better it is.

Some will say the ultra-luxury brands are not known by the masses, but then they're probably not as successful in revenue or profit terms as those such as Rolex or Rolls Royce which are popular and aspirational for the masses.

There are 3 primary characteristics that make a luxury product.

1. Symbolic Depiction of Heritage:

All of them tell a story of a rich heritage of the brand, and the brand being over 100 years old. How they have preserved the core carefully over generations. The symbolism will also come in the form of pictures of the Founder in European attire, use of Serif fonts, Roman Numerals, etc., and if you look at most such brands, they originate in countries such as Italy, France, Switzerland, and Japan. Rich culture, and they leave no opportunity to utilize it to their advantage.

2. Artificial Scarcity:

They make it super difficult for you to acquire the brand even if you have the money. Long waitlists, making you woo the retailer for months before they can attempt to arrange an item for you as a special case.

They emphasize the idea of not being able to buy it even if one has the money. You need to earn the item and yearn for it too.

3. Superior Craftsmanship and Personalization:

They'll take pride in how many hours go into putting together a single piece, and raw materials are the best of the lot, just the finest leather, berries, saffron, are used.

Here's the framework I came up with using all the points above:

Luxury Quotient = Quality Index x Heritage Index x Price Index x Scarcity Index

16. Building a Thriving Tea Business

Here's how you can make a profitable tea business in India.

I visited the Nilgiris last year (2022). It seems that a typical tea farm makes at best Rs 50k of annual return from an acre of tea gardens. Just 50k per year from an acre!

Moreover, White Tea, Green Tea and Black Tea - all come from the same tea leaves - just processed differently.

The reason green tea has picked up with the masses is because of the "health" branding associated with it.

The Indian mass tea market has a duopoly between Tata and HUL.

If you really want to crack a business here and make money, it'll be about leveraging on building a premium brand for say, white tea, or some other blend, and through the booming D2C ecosystem, sell online to a high premium paying customer.

Vahdam has a huge customer base outside the country, so tapping on such white spaces helps you make money.

Riches are in the niches.

P.S. Both Tea and Vahdam here are just examples. You either compete on cost or on differentiated value. Possibly better to go after an underserved target customer profile in a crowded market.

17. Largest Car Manufacturer

Do you know who the largest car manufacturer in the world is?

In 2020, Toyota celebrated having manufactured 9.5 Mn cars, making it the largest auto manufacturer in the world.

Now guess how many cars has 'Hot Wheels' made to date.

6 Billion Cars. 600 crores! What!!!

I know you'd say you can't compare a Hot Wheels to a Toyota, but Mattel's annual revenue continues to be USD 1 Bn per annum, and here's what I learnt from how Hot Wheels works:

› It sells 16 cars every second. And for a company which started in 1968, how are they still so relevant? It manufactures 130 new car designs every year, and their relevance is a function of continuous churning of fresh designs into the market. Over 20,000 car designs have been launched so far.

› If you think sneakers are collectibles, look at how much people spend on Hot Wheels collections. There are cars that sell in the secondary market for over 150k USD. That's well over a crore in INR.

› It's still relevant because all their designs are based on a study of recent cultures and how they can tap on them to create something that emotionally resonates and slowly pushes the purchaser towards being a collector. Much cheaper buy-in than being a collector of watches or sneakers.

› It's a tech-led company with automobile engineers who have worked at real car manufacturing companies, animators from Pixar, and most importantly, people who study cultural trends to pick emotion-evoking colors, designs and ideas.

If I were to summarise, I'd say it's a "Tech First, Human Culture led" company.

And look at how beautifully this could be the driving force for any company in the world!

18. Economics of Helicopter Rentals

If you want to buy a helicopter, it has a one-time cost of Rs 5 to 20 crores. But let's explore how chopper rental is a niche business space to be in.

If you want a helicopter on hire to capture cool video shots at your wedding, it'll cost you upwards of Rs 75,000 per hour, and easily a minimum of Rs 1,50,000/-. But your chances of being on a helicopter are more on a trip to Mata Vaishno Devi temple or Amarnath than anywhere else.

The easiest way to become a player in this space is to become an agent. A lot of celebrities and big business houses own a chopper or two, and barely use it more than 10-20 times a year, so they want folks who can be agents and find them others who would need these choppers on rent.

Here is the unit economics for running a helicopter rental.

Rental per Hour: Rs 75,000/-

Variable Costs:

› Fuel: Rs ~25,000/- per hour (35%)

› Helipad / Parking Fee per Trip: Rs ~12,000/- (15%)

› Maintenance Charges: Rs 7,500/- (10%)

A Contribution Margin of 40% is available which comes to approximately Rs 30,000 per hour. Remove another 15% for commissions, and you're left with Rs 18,750/- per hour as Margin i.e. 25%.

As for Fixed Costs:

- Salaries of Rs 4,00,000/- p.m. including Pilot and a ground staff
- Insurance & Other Maintenance Cost of Rs 1,50,000/- p.m.

That means, if each trip is about 4 hours, and you rent it out for 10 days a month, the figures would be:

- Revenue = Rs 30L p.m.
- Contribution Margin = Rs 7.5L p.m.
- Fixed Cost = Rs 5.5L p.m.
- Net Profit = 2L p.m.

which would barely cover your cost of capital.

So, you make money only if you're a broker who has the right network to get enough deals and get a 15% commission on each transaction without any investment out of your own pocket. Or work as an owneroperator, where you make at least Rs 50L p.m. in revenue from a chopper for it to be worth the risk.

Also, given how seasonal and weather dependent this can be, you'll need to find use cases across various avenues such as tourism contracts, transportation across oil rigs, islands, mountains, and in fact even as an air ambulance. As in many other businesses, there is value at scale and high frequency.

19. Business Model for Future

I talk about digital business models and have also written extensively about the 8 types of business models in my last book, *Daily Coffee & Startup Fundraising,* but lately, while analyzing platform businesses, marketplaces and D2C brands, I realize a common theme.

A lot of these new-age businesses are making losses despite reaching mass scale, having captured market share and penetrating customer reach through digital channels. And it has been done so unsustainably, that for any new player to attempt to reach their scale without burning as much money seems intimidating, and for them to turn profitable is still seemingly distant.

But let's go down to first principles.

People either buy intangibles (services, experiences, and status signals) or tangibles (goods, and status signals). Even at the core of your purchase from Amazon, Nykaa, Uber, Apple, etc., there is a hardware product. There is something tangible you can touch and feel.

And if you've followed the semiconductor industry story, I think the next sexy business would be again something old school. Again manufacturing tangible goods. Even your D2C brands have realized that the only way to make margins is through backward integration to own the manufacturing facilities.

Platform businesses like Amazon, Nykaa, Myntra, etc. are getting into manufacturing their own label of products.

A lot of these are first white-labeled contract manufactured, but after a point, the margin lies in conquering the margin at the manufacturer level.

And this return to focus on manufacturing will force businesses to stop trying to justify premium through brands and status and move the focus towards keeping prices low for customers through cost reduction.

And this focus on further cost reduction will push businesses to innovate and drive further efficiencies in manufacturing.

Just like fashion, capital markets, and human rebirth, even business models are a cycle. It moves from one to the next and back to the first. And thankfully, the world progresses because this cycle is upward-sloping.

If you're in manufacturing, know that you will continue to be the future, as long as you can bring innovations here and be the next semiconductor manufacturing monopoly for the world, or some such.

20. AI Strategy for Small Businesses/ Startups

AI models essentially use large sets of data to make accurate future predictions and thus aid efficient decision-making and execution.

As a business owner or startup, if feel you don't have enough budgets to invest in AI, which to be honest, is almost 99% of businesses, then instead of just not taking any action, try doing the following, which wouldn't cost much.

1. Know that data is the base of all AI. So if you don't have the right data collected to begin with, even if someone gives you an AI tool for free, you won't be able to use it. So begin capturing as much data as you can in your business that you don't capture currently:
    - Customer sales funnel
    - Organized customer insights
    - Revenue analysis of most selling SKUs, average order value for each customer, recurrence rate for each customer, etc.
2. Know that it's not just large data sets that we require but good data sets. In the context of food, AI and you need not just high-calorie data, but high-nutrition data. Knowing what to measure and to what extent is the first strategy to work on.
3. Play with existing no-code tech tools such as Glide, Airt-

able, Rows, Notion, ChatGPT so that you know what all is already available as an inexpensive tool that you can probably use in conjunction with some data that you're using.

There's a high probability that a large company will build AI prediction tools that businesses will be able to use for a low ticket price.

Then it'll only be a game of which business has already captured the best data.

It's Step 1 which is the most important, and honestly, not as complex as building an AI model.

21. Great Companies Have These in Common

What do companies that beat the market by almost 7 times over 15 years have in common?

Here's the biggest takeaway on the secret of phenomenal business success from the book *Good to Great* by Jim Collins.

The author analysed 1435 companies that appeared in Fortune 500, out of which only 11 made it to the list. All 11 had "Level 5" leadership at key positions incl CEO at the time of transformation.

What makes a Level 5 leader?

› Personal Humility: A compelling modesty, shunning public adulation, never boastful. Blames poor results on himself and never on other people, environment, bad luck or any external factors. Always credits success to other people, external factors and good luck.

› Ferocious Resolve and Stoic Determination: Examples of having given up millions in personal gains for the interest of the company. Fanatically driven, infected with an incurable need to produce results.

Other insights from the book:

1. 10 out of 11 good-to-great CEOs came from inside the company, whereas comparison companies tried outside CEOs six times more often.

2. There is no evidence that good-to-great companies spent

more time on long-range strategic planning than comparative companies.

3. M&A plays practically no role in the transformation from good to great.
4. Good-to-great companies were not in great industries, and some were in terrible industries.
5. Technology and technology-driven change had virtually nothing to do with igniting transformation.
6. They focused on getting the right people on their team even before knowing which direction to go in. If you begin with "who" rather than "what", you can more easily adapt to a changing world.

22. Wear Your Eye Patch!

Have you ever wondered why pirates wear eye patches? From Pirates of the Caribbean to old classics such as Treasure Island (by R.L. Stevenson) one quintessentially finds a pirate with an eye patch amongst the crew. One naturally assumes the character to have an injured or a lost eye which they are covering up or protecting through the eye patch. In reality, the reason for wearing the eye patch is completely different.

Pirates wear eye patches to prepare themselves for special circumstances. A pirate's life is a hard life, and dangers are always around the corner. One cannot predict when one would be in a swordfight with an enemy. The eye patch allows them to react quickly to dark rooms and corners. The eye already accustomed to the dark can see very well instantly, while the pupil in the other eye slowly adjusts and the eye gets accustomed to the lack of light. Imagine being pushed into a dark room during a sword fight but you gain an upper hand simply because of an eye patch.

The point I am trying to emphasize here is that if pirates thought so well about being instantly ready to deal with a blackout, why shouldn't we take inspiration and do the same with the businesses we are building? We should always be prepared for contingencies. A few examples of where contingency planning could help businesses are:

1. Backing up the website in case the server conks off
2. Realtime remote backing up of data at multiple locations
3. Having all compliance records updated for any surprise audit/scrutiny
4. Setting up two-step authentication on emails and other digital accounts
5. Ransomware insurance policy, and allied indemnity insurances

These examples are only a small glimpse of how you could be ready for unforeseen circumstances. An aware founder/individual should never take contingency planning lightly and implement as many fail-safe mechanisms as possible.

As the old adage goes, better safe than sorry.

23. Businesses Making Money During Recessions

Here's a way businesses make massive money during recessions.

It's said that during bull markets, CMOs take over companies, and push for growth. Soon, marketing budgets inflate, ads become expensive and the pay-per-click goes up 5x. You probably saw this through 2021-22: Customer Acquisition Costs for startups more than doubled, and businesses weren't getting the bang for their buck while spending on ads. Unit economics went down the drain.

And then in recessionary cycles, CFOs take over and the first thing they do is cut marketing costs to bring the highest impact on the bottom line. Oh also, people get fired, but first ad budgets are massively cut down. During the 2009 recession, the economic pullback was barely 1%, but ad spend dropped by 10%.

Now, let's look at what a business that continues to have ad money would do (owing to hopefully, them running the ship sustainably, having savings in their pockets).

When ads are cheaper, the businesses that maintain the same ad budgets suddenly are able to drive more than 2.5x sales from the same ad budget because the cost per ad word reduces. They build massive surplus in contribution margins over a period of time, ready to fight stronger when the markets come up.

This is similar to investing when markets are low, and not when markets are high. Those who keep their investments going during bear markets, actually tend to gain the most when the markets go up in a few years.

24. Lessons from the British East India Company

One of the first joint stock companies to be set up was the British East India Company. It was governed by 24 Board members who were elected by shareholders. Below them were several different levels of management, including councils, committees, and officials. There are several interesting business lessons to be learned from them.

- Efficiency: It ruled the whole of the Indian sub-continent up to Burma with less than 200 people at the London HQ.
- Perks: Free breakfasts in London, and on-site cooks (English, Portuguese and Indian) in factories, with plenty of alcohol. On holidays, that menu would swell to 16 courses and include peacocks, hares, venison and "Persian fruits" like pistachios, apricots and cherries.
- Variable Pay: In one of the most interesting ways to ensure alignment, personal trading within the employees was allowed. Which means that someone who was truly enterprising could create their own bonus structure, and if successful make enough to comfortably retire thereafter.
- High Agency: The reason looking back at this era is so interesting is that communication latencies make almost any remote management impossible. Which means we get to see the benefits (and drawbacks) of having and needing high-agency people to basically do anything with

minimal oversight.

- With the communication latency being so high, it's well nigh impossible to do anything beyond giving your employees autonomy. The natural end result of the high communication latency was that the authority atop almost always had duties of punishment rather than the ability to charge exactly what a subordinate officer should do.
- In the principles of Lean Startups, they were definitely not afraid to move fast and break things, even when things meant entire regions and huge swathes of local population.
- That said, I believe such perks and high agencies were all built on the back of loot and blood - almost like saying, if the market you're operating in is huge and bountiful, even the stupidest/cruelest of operators will thrive.
- The idea here is to take you through how the fundamentals of business and management philosophies have remained the same on a first principles basis - but hopefully, ethics and ESG should play a greater role today - despite all the greenwashing.

25. 4-S Framework for Hiring

Most hiring activity is best described as random and based on gut, which is why talent recruitment is such a pain point. More so, because people (incorrectly and shamelessly) think HR as a function does not require specialized skills to execute its deliverables.

Here are the 4-S you must incorporate in your hiring process.

1. **Scorecard:** You should have clarity on the measurable outcomes you want to job applicant to achieve in the next 1 month, 3 months, 6 months and 1 year. Have them documented for the interview, and get alignment on if they have the skills to do it, what training support would they need, and what resources would you provide to achieve these targets.

2. **Sourcing:** There has to be a process for Sourcing candidates. It could be through trusted head-hunters, or Linkedin search with pre-defined and tested keywords extracted from a clearly drafted job description with written KRA and KPIs. Also, please get hiring referrals from current team members (best source) and do background checks (mandatory) rather than simply finding candidates through job portals.

3. **Selection:** The interview process should be structured with a pre-written list of questions under the following

heads, out of which the interviewer would be trained to ask and record those that are mandatory, and those that can be picked from an entire set, such as ask any 2 from the following 10.

- Skill based questions
- Leadership experience-based questions
- Achievement based questions
- Culture-based questions
- Personal ambitions and motivations of the candidate

Not saying that drafting questions to extract genuine answers is easy, but do you have a process working towards this?

4. **Sell:** Once the right candidates are identified, sell them the idea of joining the company through:

- Market-linked pay
- Higher learning potential
- Merch and swag to build a sense of community and brag-worthiness (maybe very small impact, but do try)

Also, selling is more about listening than speaking.

26. Why Employees Leave

This is why employees leave jobs, and how eudaimonic factors can help keep them at the workplace.

I've been studying about, and discussing with clients, the reasons for why employees leave their jobs. The most common motivations seem to be the following, in ascending preferential order:

1. Money or Pay (only up to a point).
2. Social satisfaction i.e. friendships, lifestyle, relatability to the ancillaries and status of the job.
3. Wanting to challenge oneself to upskill, do something better, break the monotony… which may also result in feeling like: "I should do something of my own or be an entrepreneur."

To summarise, people want to get paid well, have a good social circle and status related to the job, but beyond those two it's the feeling of wanting to be your own boss or continuing to learn something new or finding their purpose by "creating impact" daily!

The study of happiness says that there are two kinds of happiness: hedonic (derived from pleasurable activities and experiences), and eudaimonic (derived from purpose, overcoming challenges and constant upskilling).

I feel the first two aspects of pay and status are taken care of by most employers, but the third is the trickiest to manage. And the biggest reason for stress at the workplace is that people don't feel a sense of purpose in doing the tasks, and thus a feeling of drudgery (or lack of appreciation for impact) begins to set in.

I think the following measures from employers could help:

› Hiring based on cultural fit over technical skills so that soft areas of "social" and "purpose" related motivations are prioritized for long term employer-employee relationships.

› Breeding intrapreneurship: Promoting new initiatives at work and giving employees the freedom to ideate and build new products or service verticals - like incubating startups in the same industry within the organization. InfoEdge seemingly does a great job at it.

› Setting up a Learning & Development department that focuses on constant upskilling of the employees and promoting them to newer skills and jobs rapidly.

27. How Many Freeloaders?

Derek Price was a British physicist and information scientist who found that 50% of the work is done by the square root of the total number of people who participate in the work.

This means if you have 25 people in your organization, only 5 do half the work!

For an organization of 100 people, half the work is done by just 10 people.

That means the other half is probably done by another 10 people (rough consolidation of effort).

This means 80% of the people are actually freeloading and getting paid for it. This magnifies and increases the proportion of freeloaders as organizations get bigger.

The study took birth in academia, but when tested across industries and functions, held true everywhere.

In a team of 25 salespeople, just about 5 will get more than half the sales.

You can relate this to the Pareto Principle, or the Power Law but this specific case holds true for workplace productivity measurement.

28. Family Business Issues

Every Family Business has these exact issues, and they're no less than a daily soap opera.

1. Conflict over soft issues such as:

- A feeling of one child being favoured over the other
- An undercurrent of emotional baggage over non-business related matters such as the preference of a romantic partner or spouse not liked by the parents
- Disregard for independent career choices by children

2. Conflict over ownership:

- Unclear, pooled in shareholding in a company, trust, HUF or AOP
- Parents having full ownership with no written will or conflicted view on a split with children
- Centralized control over funds makes the second generation feel powerless

3. Conflict over Strategy:

- Old ways vs new trends and tech
- No unity of command for second-level management
- Financial expansion vs ethos of the business
- Lack of respect for new ideas by the second generation

I've been a part of my family business for over a decade, and continue to play a semi-active role, juggling between some duties there along with my other ventures. Also, as a consultant, I've always looked for a resource that would put down all the problems that plague a family-run business in a framework and help find best practices for resolution.

I laid my hands on "Untangling Conflict: An Introspective Guide for Families in Business" by Dr. Janmajeya Sinha among others. Dr. Sinha is the Chairman of BCG India and has advised some of the largest family-run enterprises not just in India but internationally. The co-authors come with equal if not more credibility and experience in the space with Chinese, Japanese and other Asian family-run businesses. They've given a step-by-step guide to resolving such issues all with the help of a case study of a fictional family business, that's very relatable. Highly recommended.

29. Types of Acquirers

Most people will tell you that there are two types of buyers—Financial and Strategic.

- Financial buyers buy your business at a price (after comparing it to competition and alternative options) to hunt a bargain. They want to buy at a low price so that the amount they'll earn from the future profits of your business would be higher and they pocket gains overall.
- Strategic Buyers are bigger players in the industry who want to acquire you for non-financial concerns as well. They are interested in the geography you serve, or it helps them expand into a new vertical. Or it helps them become complete in an industry from a value chain perspective. They may offer you a higher price because there's an incentive other than just financial at play.
- The third is an Emotional Buyer. This could be say, a public company, which has huge reserves but is slowly becoming irrelevant and is unsure about how it will regain its lost glory. It just wants to try anything to be cool, young, and hip again.

An emotional buyer will often pay much more than the other types of buyers because they are miserable about their reduced relevance.

If you're looking to be acquired as a business, remember, the incentives of the acquirer are important to gauge. Once you can categorize them well among these three, you can play them best to extract maximum return on your sale.

30. Skills Stacking

Quick question for you: What will be your cumulative percentile if you get a 90th percentile in Math on the GMAT and 95th percentile in English?

Many people would think they would be around the 92nd percentile, but it may actually be the 98th percentile!!

This is because most experts in Math may not be as good at English, and vice versa. But if you're above the 90th percentile at both, then you may be in the top 2% of all test takers.

This is because it's fairly easy to be the top 10% at one thing, but darn difficult to be in the top 1%.

Which is why one of the best ways to stand out is to become the top 10% at a bunch of amazing skills. This is called *Skills Stacking*. A term coined by Scott Adams.

It works best if those skills are complementary. Imagine you're good at human psychology, no-code product building, personal branding, networking, and public speaking - you might make a successful entrepreneur with a product that captures the market and becomes a market leader.

31. Freelancing Growth

Here is how freelancing businesses are changing, and the path to go from Rs. 2 lakhs to Rs. 50 lakhs a month!

The following has been popularly called the Hyper Freelance Model, and here's breaking it down for you.

Freelancers (lawyers, designers, accountants, artists) in today's day and time need to build their business in 3 areas:

- Consulting
- Education
- Product

It works in the following manner:

1. As you work with clients as a freelance consultant, you'll naturally spot recurring pains. While you provide solutions to individual clients at an hourly rate or retainer or a fixed fee, there's a cap to how much money you can make. Most freelancers will find it really hard to go beyond Rs 5 lakh a month. That's a one-person team only. Now, let's see how this guy can scale up to several crores per annum in revenue.
2. You organize all the information you provide to clients in a structure - think FAQs, that extend to detailed course material. Now start doing B2C sales but serving multiple

people at a time rather than one - through courses.

3. Gradually, once you build a community on the back of courses and content, you must Must MUST work towards productizing that knowledge into an asset or a product, say, a book. Next, you try and automate some of the tasks all your community members need to do. Think templates, SOPs, etc. Small software and no-code tools. Then start selling those tools. Consulting builds experience but your payoff is variable to your time! With enough experience and abstraction, you share everything you know in the teaching phase. This phase creates multiple virtuous circles, notably letting you charge higher rates for your consulting activity and creating a potential audience for your first product.
4. Finally, with an audience, experience, and cash, you can remove yourself from providing services and instead sell a product that grows without you.

32. Perception Management

Do you know the definition of unhappiness?

It is the difference between your expectations and your reality - when your expectation far exceeds what's actually happening.

Now, while the above idea has enough use cases in every aspect of life, since I mostly talk about business, let's look at it from that lens.

At your job, or if you work as a freelancer or entrepreneur, you are compensated based on your performance. And performance is a function of:

1. Setting the right expectations

2. Exceeding those expectations

3. Communicating your impact to your manager/client

And remember, clients/companies pay not for value, but "perceived value".

Perception management is such an important part of work, and the term, in my view, should not be looked at as an indicator of poor culture or politics, or bootlicking. We're not in a perfect world, and managing expectations as well as communicating the value you add is a part of you marketing yourself. I see so many people complaining that they're sincere workers but others just work their way up through politics and no one sees the value they add.

Sorry, tough luck. That's an excuse in most cases for you not being able to market yourself. The day you start looking at it as a skill you need to work on rather than blaming it on others' malice, you begin to act towards it rather than think of yourself as a victim.

Part 2
Business Finance: Measure What Matters

"If you can't measure it, you can't improve it." This is a quote mostly attributed to the famed management guru Peter Drucker. Although there may be others who claim it, the point is that it's true. You indeed can't improve something you don't measure and track frequently.

In this section, I've collated notes on topics related to measuring the right things the right way. Some chapters are about plain, hard metrics that every business must track, and there are others that are more guiding principles on specific topics.

My hope, at the very least, is that this section will equip you with the right approach towards measuring data. It's obviously not possible to cover everything on this vast topic, but the specific lessons will help you build the right mindset about measuring what matters.

33. Measure What Matters

What Anil Kumble is teaching cricketers is the same as what my MBA taught me.

Spektacom is a company co-founded by Anil Kumble in 2017 and it helps batsmen find the best spot on their bat, and the angle to hit with to improve performance.

Spektacom's PowerBat is a light sticker that is stuck to the bottom of the bat. It produces graphical reports and data on the PowerBat app, including information about the power, swing, angles, and speed of the bat.

Priyank Panchal, a Gujarat player, uses the sticker to improve his performance. He says he's been able to see what was wrong with his backlift and has understood it better and improved it rather than depending on his coach's vague explanations, which he couldn't understand completely.

Vijay Madyalkar, director and head coach of batting at Just Cricket Academy in Bengaluru, provides an example of a batsman who had an issue with power-hitting. This batter was not able to find the boundary consistently, Madyalkar says. The problem baffled his coaches: they had watched over many sessions but could not pinpoint the cause. PowerBat told them exactly what they needed to know. Every time the player hit the ball, his grip twisted ever so slightly, which in turn compromised the power of the hit. It's the kind of detail that evades the naked eye. Suddenly the guy understands and starts hitting when he sees the numbers. It's a great thing, what else could you want?

And what's been my biggest takeaway from the MBA program? You can only improve what you measure!

Sounds basic, but it's surprising how many small and medium businesses in India measure nothing more than monthly sales! Businesses require measurements in HR, finance, operations, product development, and literally every other function. Most SME business owners do not even have an MIS dashboard in Excel to view weekly performance.

I'd strongly recommend all business owners switch to weekly MIS tracking rather than monthly or quarterly. When the month is over, you've already missed the bus. While cricketers are tracking data with every ball, it's unfair to look at business numbers only once a month.

34. Don't Drown

If your hands and legs were tied and you were thrown into a pool of water to drown, what would you do?

This is a common training exercise for the US Navy SEALs called drown-proofing. They are tied and thrown into a 9-foot-deep pool and must survive for 5 minutes.

Now, most people panic as soon as they hit the water. Their body moves vigorously in panic and they continue drowning, soon becoming unconscious.

Moving one's limbs doesn't help as they are tied and will not help one swim or stay up. Plus, moving frantically also burns more oxygen and makes them unconscious sooner.

The trick is to just let your body calmly sink and hit the bottom, and then just so lightly push yourself up so that you begin to rise up to the top - take a breath of air - and then descend calmly again.

What makes one win this challenge is letting go of something you don't have much control over. And the same thing applies in business when people tend to chase output metrics.

How much revenue you're hitting this month is futile to measure if you're not measuring things like - new client meetings you had; number of follow-up calls done; conversion rate of ads, etc.

Lack of identification, measure, or insight on input metrics makes you set goals that you have no idea how you'll achieve, and then do silly things to get to the output metric - drowning your goal with yourself.

Let go of output metrics, and grab a bloody hold on the input levers that drive them. That is where the moat lies.

35. Are Surveys Reliable?

How many pairs of underwear does an average Indian man own?

This anecdote used to be narrated by Prof. Harish Bijoor in our Rural Marketing class at ISB.

A consumer research company once went around asking Indian men the same question, and all would answer either 3, 4, or 5.

However, when they entered the respondent's homes to identify those pairs, they found that an average Indian man had just 1.5 pairs of underwear.

Now this tells us that user survey answers are never the best source to base business decisions on.

Companies that know their customers best validate the insights through user observation, consumer behaviour understanding, and history of ongoing consumer relationships to arrive at what would be a more refined consumer insight.

Because what consumers say is different from what consumers think, and is different from what consumers do.

Or maybe, the research company forgot to count the underwears these guys were wearing and maligned them unnecessarily.

36. Sample Size for Surveys

How many people should you survey to test your business idea or product?

As a rule of thumb, the Margin of Error (MoE) in making any inferences from a survey, depending on the number of participants, is approximately 1/square root(N).

At 10 respondents, your MoE is at ~32%

At 100 respondents, the MoE is 10%

At 200, MoE is ~7%

At 500, MoE is ~4.5%

At 1000, MoE is ~3%

This means the margin of error decreases only marginally with an increase in numbers beyond 200, but a sample size of less than 100 is bound to give you some incorrect inferences.

Thus, optimize for a respondent sample size to be between 100 to 200.

Adding more will give you more accurate results (and possibly more credibility), but the costs of conducting it may not justify the refinement in inference.

37. Build an ROI Calculator

What's the most important feature of anti-virus software?

Hint: It's not virus elimination.

It's the dialog box that tells the customer: "5 Viruses Eliminated Successfully."

When you develop a tech product for your customer (especially in the case of B2B or enterprise software), your sales increase substantially if you can show the user how much efficiency they've achieved, or cost they've saved, or the extra revenue they've generated by using your software.

The ROI calculator is the most important feature.

Decisions in enterprise software are taken by employees, who would need to know how much they've saved or made their company in monetary terms by taking a decision. What's the ROI of the decision? This impacts their appraisal, their growth in the company, as well as gives them the comfort of having made a good decision.

So no matter what product you build and deliver. If you can build an ROI calculator for the customer, it increases the value to your customer substantially with this minor difference.

38. Turn Fixed Cost into Variable

Here's a business idea for you to think about. I believe it has massive potential.

What if you could break a fixed cost into variable costs for a customer? It'll save them considerable capital expenditure upfront and reduce business risk because they will only pay for what they use.

This is where banks tried dabbling with vehicle leasing businesses: Instead of buying the car, lease it. But let's see where else this applies.

Amazon launched its AWS service, making cloud storage and server infrastructure a variable cost instead of fixed.

There are enough furniture providers and home furnishing businesses that say you can pay to use the furniture per month rather than buying it upfront.

But here's a catch. For any such business, it leads to massive upfront costs, where they invest in such capex themselves, which they try to earn rentals out of. Call it tokenization, if you may.

As a business, a real business model is created when you take assets of suppliers (owned by others) and build a marketplace to tokenize them for end users. The best example is Uber.

Some will say Indians don't pay for subscriptions. But what if your target customers are young businesses (so-called startups)? Would they sign up for something that turns their fixed cost into a variable?

Think:

1. Branding cost as a variable expense (based on # unit sales)
2. Accounting cost as a variable expense (based on # of entries)
3. Rental cost as a variable expense (# of in-office man days) - like WeWork hot passes?

39. Restaurant Metrics

If you want to open a restaurant, what financial metrics should you keep in check? Let's look at them.

- Food and Material costs should be less than 30% of revenue
- Rent should be within 20% of revenue
- Utilities (electricity, water, fuel) could be another 10%
- Salaries to staff should be within 20%
- Other overheads including marketing and commissions no more than 10% of revenue

This way, you get to make at least 10% profit (EBITDA) on your revenue. If you're not even making that, why are you in this business? Unfortunately, most restaurants don't even make this and just survive at break even.

Check the average revenue of other restaurants in the same market or mall before opening the restaurant. If 90% of the average revenue does not cover your costs as per the structure above, rethink your business model.

Also remember that QSR, casual dining, fine dining, and cloud kitchens work on different cost structures. Do not compare with models different than yours.

40. Managing Low Gross Margin Business

Finance hack: What to do if you are in a low gross margin business?

There are 2 ingredients to earning a good financial return in your business. The first is a profit margin and the second is velocity. Most people understand the first, but let's understand the second.

Velocity is the speed with which things move in your business. How quickly do you purchase, stock that material in the inventory, get sales for it, recover your money and start the process again?

Imagine a street vendor is in a 10% profit margin business, but has taken a loan from a lender at 2% per month. That means he's taken a loan at 24% p.a. for a business that makes just a 10% margin on sales! How will he pay the 24% p.a. by making just a 10% profit?

Well, the answer lies in the velocity.

If he can keep churning his inventory, selling it quickly, making his 10%, and then use that money to buy and sell again and keep making lots of 10% through high velocity in his stock sales, he'll easily be able to accumulate a lot of 10% in a year and cover the 24% borrowing cost.

This is very simplistically explaining it, but did you know that Walmart has 360 average turns of toilet paper a year? That's like they sell all their toilet paper inventory every day, and use the cash recovered to fund the next day's inventory.

The *return* you make in business is a function of gross margin *(profit)* and *velocity.*

If you have lower margins, go for the highest possible velocity and turn your inventory around multiple times a month. Keeping 45-60 days' inventory at all times will kill your business. Try and come down to just 10 days of inventory, and keep churning it.

You need to ensure that your Return on Capital Employed is more than your Cost of Capital. It's all by balancing margins and velocity together.

41. What Marketplace Stakeholders Want

Do you know what are the commission and margin rates across industries?

For farm produce - fruits and veggies, wholesalers keep 5% while retailers keep 35%, leaving 55-60% for farmers.

In FMCG, wholesalers, stockists, and retailers, collectively keep just 15-20% and about 75-80% goes to the manufacturer.

In Pharma, the margins can go up to 35%, collectively split across retailers and distributors, and the manufacturer keeps 60-65%.

This actually tells you that across industries, 25-35% is a reasonable margin paid for distributors and retailers, traditionally.

Now, you may say that even big online marketplaces take a similar percentage as their share of the Gross Merchandise Value (GMV), so where is the value-add for the seller?

The value-add is not in the margin.

If you're building a B2C marketplace online, remember that the real value-add from you is in combining the stack of deliverables in one place for more seamless transactions. For the suppliers, help with solving the following:

› New customer discovery

› Geographical expansion of products

- Tech support / ERP implementation & systems
- Faster receipt of payments
- Loan & financing options
- Dealing with just one intermediary who defines margins and not pressures from a stack of different brokers (more the players, more the variables in pressure)

As for the buyers, build a stack that ensures:

- Wider variety of options
- Financing and EMI
- Faster deliveries and logistics
- Pooling in purchases from different vendors
- Seamless payment options

42. Average Revenue Per Order or User

Content creators have have had a difficult time over the last few months of 2022.

Right up to Diwali of 2022, a lot of creators with a following of over 500k on social media were earning Rs 5 lakhs (USD 6k) monthly through brand deals and influencer marketing campaigns.

However, given the recessionary pressures on companies and mass layoffs, marketing budgets have been slashed drastically, and the value of brand deals in the market is down in 2023 to just 10% of what it was in early 2022. It's none of their fault. It's just a market cycle.

This also tells you that in India, it's easy to collect a crowd of people, but hard to get them to pay you even a rupee each. The success metric of an influencer is no longer the number of followers they have, but the average revenue per follower.

And the same metrics have taken meaning across all businesses and startups. Much more than daily or monthly active users, the metric on which valuations now depend is Average Revenue per User (ARPU).

Your community in business may be worthless if you can't convert that into revenue. Please start tracking ARPU over DAUs and MAUs - because vanity metrics are out, cash flow metrics are in.

43. CODS - Customer Obsession, Delight, and Satisfaction

You measure COGS in your business, but do you measure CODS?

CODS is an abbreviation for Customer Obsession, Delight, and Satisfaction.

Satisfaction is when something meets your expectations.

Delight is when something exceeds your expectations and pleasantly surprises you.

Obsession is when you can't stop thinking about something.

While customer satisfaction is a baseline measure - it's adding delight and being customer-obsessed (cue Amazon) that actually leads to longer customer retention, repeat purchases, and a higher lifetime value (LTV).

Here's how you measure these metrics:

› **C-SAT** is a measure of the Customer Satisfaction score, which asks the customer to rate if they've been satisfied with the experience on a scale of 1 to 5. The key lies in knowing when to measure this. Would you measure this when the customer places an order on your website, or after receiving the order?

› **NPS** is Net Promoter Score or how likely is the customer to refer you to others within their network. Where on a scale of 1 to 10, 10 means most likely and 1 means least likely.

Customers marking 9 and 10 are called Promoters. 1-6 are Detractors, and 7-8 are Neutrals.

Your NPS is (% Promoters - % Detractors), which should ideally be above 50. In 2018, Netflix had an NPS of 64, PayPal scored 63, Amazon 54, Google 53, and Apple 49.

› **Retention and Repeat Rates:** For apps, +25% retained users after 90 days of install is phenomenal, and 10% should be the preferred baseline for a good product.

For tangible products, you check the frequency of repeat orders as per natural buying frequency - and you do that individually for cohorts onboarded from similar times or campaigns to see which types of cohorts have stuck around and those which have fizzled off.

Using public product reviews and social media comments as a metric may give results skewed more toward detractors as people tend to publish more about negative experiences publicly than positive ones. But reduced complaints could be a measure of reaching the baseline.

Be obsessed with your customer, and always aim for delight!

44. Contra-COGS

If you're a D2C brand, you need to know what is Contra-COGS while selling through Amazon.

COGS means Cost of Goods Sold. If you sell a product for Rs 100, and the cost of such goods to you is Rs 40, you have a COGS of 40%, simplistically.

If you sell products to first one of Amazon's "sister entities", like what was Cloudtail, Appario, etc., then you become a vendor to, say, a Cloudtail, and Cloudtail sells your products further to end customers. Here, your selling price to Cloudtail becomes COGS for Cloudtail, right?

Now, let's say Cloudtail buys this product from you for Rs 80 and then sells it to the end customer for Rs 100, that means Cloudtail makes a profit of Rs 20 on the sale. But if you decide to offer more discounts to the end customer and want Cloudtail to sell the product at a cheaper price of Rs 90, then the loss of Rs 10 in profit that Cloudtail will incur, it will recover from you in the form of "Contra-COGS"

Such Contra-COGS charges can come in various forms, but is essentially a way for marketplaces like Amazon to ensure a certain minimum profit on every sale through their platform, even if the end customer is offered a discount.

Here's the kicker though.

In some cases, if you sell the same product at a lower price on any platform other than Amazon, then you may need to pay the differential to Amazon as a penalty or "Contra-COGS" as they would call it too.

45. Burn Multiple

What should be your startup's Burn Multiple?

As marketing spends are curtailed in a bear market, the growth metrics tracked in Financial MIS in startups should change from "growth metrics" to "efficient growth metrics", i.e. we don't just track the absolute growth in the number of active users or top line sales, but the cost or burn at which such active users or top line is being achieved.

Burn Multiple = Net Burn / Net New ARR

Here, Burn Multiple measures how much money has been burnt to get new Annual Recurring Revenue (or active users). It is a concept popularized by David Sacks (VC at Craft Ventures; and Founding COO of PayPal).

As an example, if you spend Rs 5 lakhs to get a new client contributing to an ARR of Rs 2 lakhs, that means the Burn Multiple is 2.5x.

Given how much jugglery startups are prone to in removing costs from unit level costs to keep gross margins and contribution margins high, by moving them to admin and general expenses - the Burn Multiple plugs that issue for VCs as they like to look at the total net burn instead of just unit-level costs.

As per Andreessen Horowitz (a16z), a good Burn Multiple for SaaS companies is as under, classified based on ARR:

ARR < $10M... 1.1x Multiple (Median is 1.6x)

$10M < ARR < $20M... 0.8x Multiple (Median is 1.4x)

$25M < ARR < $75M... 0.5x Multiple (Median is 0.7x)

ARR > $75M... 0x (Median is 0.5x)

Measures to control the Burn Multiple:

- Focus on increasing engagement and sales of high LTV cohorts
- Double down on distribution channels with the highest contribution margins (CM)
- Curtail sales through low CM channels
- Hold on spending on Brand Marketing

46. AARRR Test

Investors evaluate whether your customers pass the AARRR Test!

If you have a digital product and you plan to tell investors your traction in the form of total downloads or total visitors to your websites, you may be in trouble.

Investors want to see the entire funnel of how you activate customers, which you do by measuring them through the AARRR test. The deeper down the funnel you go, the higher your startup's value.

A - Acquisition - No. of Visitors or Downloads

A - Activations - Those who viewed for over 2 mins, or made over 3 clicks, or signed up for the newsletter

R - Retention - Those who opened your email, or visited again within the week

R - Referral - Those who referred others to visit or join, or shared the link with others

R - Revenue - Those who actually paid

Anyone can burn money and get visitors or downloads, it's going deeper down the funnel that has value.

Fun fact - you can build this framework for your brick-and-mortar, traditional bootstrapped business as well. And you must!

47. 70% Rule: Launch, Fail, Iterate Fast

It took me 2 months to write 90% of my first book *Daily Coffee & Startup Fundraising*, and another 2 months to complete the balance 10%.

I was getting so impatient during the process even though I know the average time to get a manuscript ready is ~15 months. But shipping out early is what I wanted to optimize for. And Wyzr, my publisher, promised that start to out-in-the-store will be done in less than 5 months.

I was proud of what we'd achieved, but I was studying standard deviations today and found this interesting insight, which applied to my book-writing process.

› 1 Std Dev is ~68%

› 2 Std Dev is ~95%

› 3 Std Dev is ~99.9%

If it takes 1.5 months to write 90% of the book (being ~1.5 Std Dev), it'll take another 1.5 months to get to 99.9%

This means that the final 10% takes just as much time as the first 90% - not because I was being impatient about the process, but because that's how the world mostly functions.

I dug deeper to find this blog by Taylor Pearson, who talks about the 70% Rule, and I quote:

"As you get closer and closer to finished, it starts taking much longer to make progress.

"The mistake most people and organizations make is that they think 'Well, I want to do my best work so I want to get it to 99%.'

"What this ignores is the opportunity cost. If it takes you 3 months to get 70% of the way finished, are you better off spending another 6 months getting to 99% or getting two other projects to 70%?

"For entrepreneurs and startups, particularly early stage, the answer is almost always the latter, getting three projects to 70% is better than getting one to 99%.

"Quantity is a quality on its own."

So, aim for 70%, launch faster, fail faster, iterate faster. Because software and intangibles afford us the luxury to make mistakes which may be easily reversible, which wasn't possible when goods used to be tangible and produced in mass batches in factories.

48. North Star Metrics

Have you noticed that if you see right while riding a bicycle, the bicycle will automatically start drifting to the right?

This is why they say it's important where you focus your attention. In business, that focus is on the North Star Metric.

There can be 6 types of North Star metrics:

1. Revenue-Based (ARR, MRR, GMV)
2. Customer Growth Based (DAU: Daily Active User, MAU, Paying Users, Market Share)
3. Consumption-Based (No. of Messages sent, No. of Rides)
4. Engagement Growth (Average time spent / DAU)
5. Growth Efficiency (LTV / CAC i.e. Lifetime Value / Customer Acquisition Cost)
6. User Experience (NPS: Net Promoter Score)

Which metric to focus on depends on your business model and stage of business. You can read in depth about these business models in my book *Daily Coffee & Startup Fundraising*.

49. Uber's North Star Metric

What do you think is Uber's North Star Metric? Most people get it wrong.

A North Star metric is that one number that everyone in the business chases to increase - for app-based products, it could be downloads or active users, for software providers, it could be recurring revenue, for marketplaces, it could be gross merchandise value.

When a company like Uber was to launch, most people would think that the North Star Metrics would be two: number of rides.

But Uber figured that the correct metric to measure was the ETA - Estimated Time to Arrival.

It tried that there should always be enough drivers and customers available that the average ETA should be less than 10 mins.

If there aren't enough customers, drivers will drop off and not care to be on the app. If there aren't enough drivers, customers would drop off.

The metric changes based on the stage of the company. Have you thought hard through this while establishing your North Star metric?

50. New Metric to Measure Growth

Coronavirus gave a new metric to startups to measure growth.

Do you remember how experts on TV used to say that the coronavirus has an R0 (R-naught) of 2.

This R0 value of 2 means that one infected person will infect two more, which means there will be an exponential growth in the number of infected people and it will spread like wildfire.

So R0 < 1 means the virus will die soon as each person will infect less than one person.

R0 = 1 means the growth of the virus will be linear, and

R0 > 1 means the growth will be crazy

In the context of business, R0 should be looked at how many referrals you can get from your existing users or customers. Here, R0 is a function of the number of people referring multiplied by the actual conversion rate from such referrals.

Referral schemes are the best way to reduce customer acquisition costs, and if a business chooses to ignore a strategy for it, they're missing out on viral growth.

Why do you think I say, "Share it with someone who may need it" at the end of all my social media videos? Because the biggest call to action for your business is getting people who know you to bring you many more.

Referral strategies include referral incentives and discounts, which make it easy for your customers to refer you. Either through a customized link that automatically goes through WhatsApp or a share button on a social media app.

51. Growth Rate v/s Stick Rate

If you're a consumer app or a B2C product, you may begin to start talking about the Growth Rate of user acquisition as one of the North Star metrics while speaking with investors.

However, what matters much more than Growth Rate is the Stick Rate that measures the stickiness of your product, or retention, or how much time users are spending on your app.

Because investors know that you can buy growth, but you cannot buy retention - and retention as a cohort metric is more important to track than just user downloads growth.

Show organic growth, as that may be sustainable as it's not bought.

At the first stage of funding, someone may value you basis total users, but at the next stage, they will only value you if your retention is better than the industry average - say, over 25% after 90 days.

52. Benchmarks for Business Growth Rate

What should be the growth rate of your company, or how fast should your business grow?

Growth rates are a result of several factors such as industry growth rate, GDP growth rate, stage of the company (early/mature), access to capital, desired return on equity, etc. However, let's look at some broad thumb rules that can help you determine if your business growth is reasonable or not.

- **GDP Benchmark:** You should ideally grow at a minimum of 3X the GDP growth rate of your country. This can be assumed at about 5% p.a., so your business should ideally grow at about 15% p.a. at the very least.
- **Inflation Benchmark:** If the inflation rate is at 6%, you should ideally grow at an annual growth rate at least 2x of that to actually, meaningfully grow your business. The same applies to your industry growth rate.
- **Return on Equity Benchmark:** If you expect the stock market to give you a return of 12% p.a. on your investment, ideally the return on investment in your own business should be higher because shares give you passive income. Your own business requires active effort, so best if it's double the return. Thus, for unlisted privately held businesses, given the risk profile, an annual return of 24% is expected.

- **IPO Benchmark:** Listed companies around the world are expected to grow on an average of upwards of 20% in the year in which they IPO.
- **Y Combinator Benchmark:** Paul Graham says that at the absolute early stage of startups accepted to YC, they're expected to grow at 5% per week!

The metric for growth for most businesses may be different: some may want more revenues or market share or some other operating metric, but in the real sense, it has to be net cash inflows, i.e. actual cash taken home net of all expenses—that must grow every year.

53. Customer Carrying Cost

Customer Carrying Cost is something most startups don't calculate.

CAC or Customer Acquisition Cost is mostly calculated to the point of getting a person to come on the platform, download the app or make their first purchase.

But most internet business models are such that the profit from the first sale is not enough to cover the cost of acquisition, which is why metrics such as LTV/CAC aim to indicate the total return one can generate from the customer over a longer period.

If you've built a tech product, you know the evil of churn, and most customers acquired will fall off the app or the product in a couple of weeks or a month to never come back and make a purchase again.

Startups then spend on customer engagement to ensure such users become active users and don't fall off. They then hope these active users convert to paying users or buy again someday.

All costs spent on building such engagement is called Customer Carrying Cost (CCC), and it adds to the Customer Acquisition Cost.

Ideally, ratios to monitor should be LTV/(CAC+CCC) instead of just LTV/CAC.

54. Why Bank Branches Exist

You probably have no idea why your closest bank branch even exists anymore.

A bank branch does not exist to help you with RTGS/NEFT/ATM or cash withdrawals, etc. All of that can now be done through online banking and they possibly can't waste so much real estate over these matters.

The main purpose of your closest bank branch is to make sales and get people to open more accounts. Why?

Because the lifetime value (LTV) of a banking customer is massive. Almost 10 years on average. How many times do you change your account even if you think you have an account with the worst bank with pathetic service?

By some estimates, churn rates for customers are in single digits - barely 8% of people leave the bank in a year - compare that to 75% churn for digital products in 3 months.

And having this physical presence helps them open more accounts - which means future sales of loans, credit cards, insurance, mutual funds, and more.

This is a major reason why after-sale service or customer service at a bank is mostly rated to be sub-par. That's not their job! Their job was to get you to open an account - and then make you buy more financial products than to irritate them with requests of sending you a copy of your statement again.

Even the physical layout of a branch is set up to just make sales.

Your relationship manager has been made to learn scripts by heart on why your bank's mutual fund performs better than any other bank - or why the insurance scheme is the best ever in the world!

Your bank branch acts like an investor building a portfolio of accounts, out of which a few will create massive incomes for them.

And what are the best kinds of customers to attract?

1. Doctors, who earn a lot of money, but have no time to manage it, and will probably go ahead with what the "relationship manager" recommends.

2. Retirees, because they've got funds saved over the years, and if you can talk and build a relationship with a retired person well, you can convince them to take an insurance or a mutual fund.

3. Not small businesses, but individuals with savings, or corporate accounts.

55. Most Profitable in the Value Chain

Do you know who makes the maximum profit margin in the automobile business in the entire value chain?

Most people list the value chain as comprising the manufacturer (OEM), the distributor, and the dealership.

Studies of international industry averages say that manufacturers may make about 7.5% and dealerships would make about 5%.

However, the maximum profit margins in the value chain are made by vehicle financing, vehicle leasing, insurance, and second-hand car sales - all could be upwards of 10%.

With this, we see that the pattern of revenue concentration in the industry may be very different from the pattern of profit concentration.

This is called profit pool analysis - and helps a business decide which part of the value chain they should focus on to make more profits, even though revenues may be menial. For example, significant profit margins for car manufacturers are through accessories.

But profit pools are not stagnant - they keep shifting ever so often as more players come in to take a higher share. I believe EVs may shift that to battery companies or Battery as a Service (BaaS) companies.

This acts as a segue for me to reiterate what a16z and Andrew Chen have spoken about every company eventually becoming a FinTech company through embedded finance because they'll make the most money on the financing part of the transaction.

This is a major reason why BNPL, credit agencies, and fintechs are booming - where most users don't even realize how much money is made off of their transactions and the cash backs are measly in comparison to actual profits.

Now, evaluate it from a computer industry perspective. Hardware is the least profitable, even for companies like Apple. It's the service, subscription, and platform stack that makes the highest amount of profit. The hardware is just the bait to get you into the ecosystem.

56. Growth, Engagement and Retention Benchmarks

I was shocked to learn these benchmarks of monthly growth and retention rates (after a VC analyzed over 100 social apps), and I feel most Indian apps will fail to make the cut.

Andreesen Horowitz has done a detailed benchmarking on growth, engagement and retention numbers considering hundreds of early-stage social media apps to come up with the following benchmarks. To my mind, these can be applied with some modification to communities being built by startup founders for their D2C/SaaS startups as well.

Growth in Daily Active Users (DAU):

- 20% monthly is okay
- 35% monthly is good
- 50% monthly is great

Ideally, almost all of this growth should come organically. This is because social apps often can't monetize until later, so they don't have as much cash to burn on paid marketing. More intuitively, social apps should be inherently viral, with users wanting to invite their friends to make the experience even better.

If more than 10-20% of your users are coming from paid sources in the early stages, you'll likely want to rethink your acquisition strategy.

Engagement may be measured through the ratio: DAU / MAU, with broad benchmarks as follows:

- 25% is okay
- 40% is good
- 50% is great

Another metric to look at for engagement is the L-ness curve.

This metric looks at the distribution of users by number of days active over a certain time period, and can be measured on either a weekly or monthly basis. For example, on a weekly basis, how many of your WAUs are active one day per week, two days per week, three days per week, and so on?

L5 or active 5 days in a week ratio should be at least 30%, good at 40%, and great at 50%.

Now let's look at retention, which is measured as and called n-day retention. For example - if you have 100 users sign up for your app today, and 25 of those users use the app 30 days from now, your day 30 retention is 25%. "Great" benchmark for n-day retention is 70% at d1, 50% at d7, and 30% at d30.

So, the higher your n count is, or the longer your time period of measurement is, the more valuable your metrics are.

57. 1-in-60 Rule for Financial Models and MIS

The 1-in-60 rule for financial models and MIS.

The rule has been adopted from the world of aviation, and it states that a 1-degree error in direction will cause an airplane to miss its target by 1 mile for every 60 miles flown.

This framework instills the importance of real-time course corrections as you pursue growth and progress toward your goals. Here's how it applies in business, especially startups.

Most Financial MIS in business are created on a monthly basis. MIS reviews are necessary on a weekly basis, especially for startups to evaluate metrics like weekly ROAS, CAC, Revenues, DAUs, etc.

Your three-year financial model for investors is going to be junk, and they know it, which is why, focus on building a financial planning spreadsheet in which you can change inputs each week/month to see what kind of outputs in metrics you'll get if you keep progressing that way. It helps think through revised targets, have a real-time assessment of variance, and have a realistic idea of current burn rates and runway.

58. Remove Lucky Spikes

Trend lines are an important tool to show growth over a period of time. However, if you manage growth in a business - be it user growth or revenue growth or transaction growth, you know that a lot of times, it's the spikes in performance on a few days that take up the average rather than systematic consistent improvement in business processes.

And while such spikes help show a good performance in the short term, the person responsible for the metric knows that it was a one-off lucky event or a seasonal jump, and maybe such numbers may not show up in the next week or month.

So to remove the effect of such short-term spikes that can cloud the judgment of the management and make them believe it's a systematic process improvement, it's important to change the trend lines to trailing 6 weeks or trailing 3 months. Such trend lines mostly remove the impact of short-term spikes by averaging them out over a longer period to show actual progress and improvement.

59. 3-Step Framework for Data Analysis

Analyzing and inferring data is a skill, but presenting it is an even more valued skill because it's the presentation of analysis that drives decisions and not the mere process of analyzing data. Quite often the analyst who works on the data glosses over the trials and tribulations of the slog they have put in only to lose grip of the audience and miss out on driving impact as a follow-up of the analysis.

While presenting any analysis, use the following framework to present your argument.

1. Setup
2. Conflict
3. Resolution

› Your data (in the form of graphs, line charts, pie charts, trend lines, etc) should set the right context through the "setup" of the prevailing situation.

› After explaining the status quo, you explain the "conflict/anomaly/inflection point" that broke the trend or the status quo.

› Thereafter, you present the "resolution" or the superstar solution that changed the situation for the better.

For example, if you're talking about startup fundraising trends in the past few years, you'll present data on how EdTech secured massive funding across 2020-2021, out of which the highest spend of such VC money was on Customer Acquisition Cost (CAC). This is the context.

Why was the CAC rising? Because of inflation, and more VC funds competing for the same users across the same digital channels (Meta, Google) through their investments in EdTech, FinTech, and D2C. That's the conflict.

How does a business break out of this? An EdTech called PhysicsWallah had lower CAC than all of its competition because of its content-first strategy. That was the exception or the "resolution".

And then one can drive the point on how content marketing can help reduce CAC for a better Return on Ad Spend (ROAS) in EdTech.

So whenever you're required to present data, be it in a pitch deck, investor meeting, or a company all-hands, just follow the Setup-Conflict-Resolution framework.

60. Net Dollar Retention

NDR or Net Dollar Retention is an important growth metric for most businesses. Here is how you can measure it.

Net Dollar Retention (NDR) is a metric used to measure how much revenue a company retains from its existing customers over a period of time. It is calculated by taking the revenue generated from existing customers at the end of a period and dividing it by the revenue generated from those same customers at the beginning of the same period, factoring in any upsells, cross-sells, or downgrades that may have occurred.

The formula for Net Dollar Retention is:

NDR = (Ending Revenue from Existing Customers – Churn + Upselling or Cross-selling to Existing Customers)/ Beginning Revenue from Existing Customers

Where:

Ending Revenue from Existing Customers = Revenue generated from existing customers at the end of the period

Churn = Revenue lost from existing customers during the period

Beginning Revenue from Existing Customers = Revenue generated from existing customers at the beginning of the period.

NDR is different from measuring Annual Recurring Revenue (ARR) or Monthly Recurring Revenue (MRR) because it takes into account any upsells or cross-sells that may have occurred during the period, whereas ARR and MRR only measure the total revenue generated from existing customers at a given point in time.

It's measured as a percentage, so you should of course aim for an NDR of above 100%. SaaS companies going for IPO have an average of 107% NDR as per some reports.

An example of NDR would be if a company selling mint-flavoured dog food had an NDR of 150%. This would mean that their existing customers are not only continuing to buy the dog food, but they're also buying more of it, perhaps because their dogs have become addicted to the flavor. This is a hypothetical example, but given how pet adoption is on the rise in the country, it could very well be a reality.

Make sure your NDR is performing well because it certainly indicates a strong and healthy business.

61. Analyzing Financial Statements

Here are the 3 things I analyze when I review any company's financial statements.

1. Vertical Analysis

2. Horizontal Analysis

3. Key Metrics

Vertical Analysis involves looking at the numbers as a percentage to a baseline number.

For example, in a P&L statement, most expense numbers are analyzed as a percentage of sales. This is done to keep expenses within reasonable benchmark percentages. E.g. Why has raw material expense increased beyond 35% of sales?

Although for a Balance Sheet, it's looking at an asset or liability as a percentage of the total assets or liabilities. For example, why is the inventory value constantly increasing as a percentage of the total current assets?

Horizontal Analysis is when we compare data in this period with that of previous periods. It's a trend analysis across periods.

› What is the growth rate of sales?

› Why are sales not increasing at the same growth rate as the increase in marketing expenses?

- Why are receivables from customers as a percentage of sales increasing every quarter?

Key Metrics are the primary 4-5 things you would want to evaluate to check the health of your business based on the objective the business is trying to achieve, and your industry/type of business model.

As an example, it could be any of the following:

- Gross Margin %
- EBITDA %
- Sales Growth Rate %
- Revenue per Employee for Service companies
- Burn Multiple (how much are you burning to earn Re 1 of revenue) for early-stage startups
- Rule of 40 (Sales Growth Rate % + Net Profit %) for SaaS
- Cash Flow from Operating Activities

Part 3

Sales & Marketing: Let Them Know, Make Them Buy

"The aim of marketing is to know and understand the customer so well the product or service fits them perfectly and sells itself." - Peter Drucker (again).

Even though most of the work I do falls in the domain of finance, I have to admit it's marketing that I'm most fascinated by. It's a perfect combination of art and science. It's equally a game of numbers and creativity, and the two are almost always connected. This is one department of the organization that needs to have a healthy diversity of individuals and backgrounds to obtain the best results. Ultimately, good marketing is the difference between a customer paying a premium for the same product that may have otherwise sold at par with its alternatives.

This section contains some fascinating insights into marketing, consumer behaviour, branding, and pricing. Like other sections, we haven't explained the basics of sales and marketing that get taught in colleges but covered a lot of things that colleges should teach but don't.

I enjoyed working on this section the most. I hope you find the chapters enjoyable and insightful as well.

62. #1 Factor That Determines Success

Do you know the number 1 factor that determines your success in business, relationships and most things in life?

It's Trust, and how trustworthy people perceive you to be. And once you learn this equation for trust, you begin to evaluate all your actions on these factors.

Trust = (Credibility + Reliability + Authenticity) / Perception of Self Interest

Your trust increases with your credibility, reliability and authenticity but decreases if people think you're doing an action for your own good. Increases when they think you're doing it for the benefit of others.

Credibility is if you're qualified, experienced and skilled to do something.

Reliability increases through consistent behaviour.

Authenticity is you being yourself and not doing something to be falsely perceived as what you're not.

This is not an original framework, it's something I've read time and again. I believe it was framed by Harvard Business School professor, David Maister.

63. Don't Sell Ice to Eskimos

Will you try selling ice to Eskimos?

You know how they say a great salesperson is someone who can sell ice to Eskimos. But a great business person is one who would realise that eskimos want heaters more than they want ice.

And the person with that realisation will end up making much more money than the one selling ice and showing off his selling skills.

The core idea here is that way too often, businesses are focused on selling what they have as an existing product or service, and not focusing on what are the new problems of their existing customers which they can quickly build for, supply and make a hefty profit.

Sell what customers want to buy, and not what you have to sell!

64. Using Keywords Smartly

What would you pay for a black Nike t-shirt? And for the same quality t-shirt without any logo?

I ask this question often in some of the Finance classes I teach and mostly get answers along the lines of - Rs 1500 for the Nike and Rs 500 for the other.

And then I tell the class about a brand called March Tee that sells plain solid t-shirts for Rs 1500 onwards, with no logo, no branding, nothing. Just available in 3 solid colours and that's all.

It's seemingly profitable, does over Rs 12 crores of sales per annum, is bootstrapped with just one angel investor at inception, and sells only from its website. No marketplace sales for discovery.

If you ask D2C founders, they'll tell you about how selling from your own website is extremely costly from a Customer Acquisition Cost perspective.

If that's so, how did March Tee run its performance advertising for it to be not just sustainable, but profitable?

If you had to pick words to run ads on Instagram and Google to promote and tell consumers about March Tee, what words would you pick? Organic, solid, tshirt, soft, cotton, plain, premium, luxury, brandless, no logo?

They picked "foreign travel" and "art films". These words have nothing to do with their product, but everything to do with their target customer persona.

The cost of digital ads is a function of the number of bidders, commonly used search words, etc. This was their way of picking words that were not being bid on (Covid times) but still defined their target group extremely well.

And that's how marketing is supposed to be done. March Tee is a phenomenal case study with amazing branding and seemingly, great financial numbers too. I read about it on The Hard Copy blog(thehardcopy.co).

65. Create a Religion

What can businesses learn from temples? What happens when you walk into a temple?

You are probably amazed by the architecture at the gate, the adornments on the wall, the structure of the deity. Walk in further and you begin to smell incense. Maybe flowers, maybe sandalwood. It's comforting. You begin to associate that smell with the deity. Further in, you hear hymns, maybe a cymbal, a dholki, the pundit chanting praises in a song. You make a mental note, probably recommend the bhajan to your mother, find it for her to play on YouTube. You then bow down on your knees, put your head to the ground in reverence. You touch the altar and take that touch back to your forehead. Maybe the pundit puts a tilak on your forehead.

While exiting, they give you a little morsel of Prasad. Sugar pellets offered to the lord, or maybe charanamrita. Things you associate with that specific temple. Like Gurudwaras give you kadha prasad.

The institution appealed to you visually, aurally, through smell, touch and taste. All 5 senses. You associate those visuals, smells, tastes with that temple - it's distinct for a Vishnu Temple, than it is for a Gurudwara, than it is for a Church or a Mosque.

If businesses want to be loved and revered by their customers, they need to attempt and create not a brand but a religion. Something that's appealing to all 5 senses of the customer. The logo looks great, the touch on the packaging and product is premium, there's a fond smell in the store, a jingle you associate with it. Even services find a way to send you a loyalty card or a kit to appeal to touch which they otherwise may not be able to.

Are you creating a brand or a religion?

66. Guerilla Marketing

How did you first get to know about Red Bull?

I saw it first when during my college fest about 12 years ago (2010), a few attractive women were giving out cans to everyone who'd approach them and ask for it, for free!

Many years later, while at ISB, I remember, they gave away free cans before the first term exams so that people could gulp some and stay up the whole night. And then we also roped them in to dole out a few hundred cans during the placement season.

Their target audience had majorly been 18 to 35-year-old men, which is why they handed them out for people to try at fests, cafes, libraries, sporting events, and what not. Who doesn't recognize their association with extreme sports - Red Bull Cliff Diving World Series, Red Bull Air Race, Red Bull Crashed Ice and stunts like stratos space diving project?

In fact, they used to also place heaps of empty cans in and around dust bins outside nightclubs to make the drink seem extremely popular. That's Guerilla Marketing.

So here are a few questions to check off for your business' marketing strategy.

› Are you present online and physically at all places where your customer is present?

- Are you doing something newsworthy to get free press coverage?
- Have you found a compelling way to make your customers try your product for free?

67. Unpaid Marketing

How many man-hours of work do you get done from others without paying for it?

Try answering this question as a test to know how defensible your business is from a community or network effects standpoint.

Let me explain.

Social media websites get creators to make content for their platform without paying for most of the content. They're getting media at no production cost of their own.

Has your business built a community on Discord, WhatsApp, Telegram, or some such platform where your existing customers interact with each other to solve each other's questions and save your time from answering all questions yourself, thus saving you cost for after-sales services?

As a professional (doctor/lawyer/accountant/designer), do you have a group of peers where you post a problem, and the community gives you the answers, thus saving you time to research for the starting point of the solution yourself?

Developer communities are known very well to collaborate online to write code and solve each other's problems.

And when it comes to marketing, remember that word-of-mouth marketing is also a form of marketing man-hours that you don't directly pay for.

68. Designing Word-of-Mouth

How do you enable word-of-mouth marketing by design?

Krispy Kreme in the US prices its donuts in a way that a dozen is just slightly more expensive than buying 4, which prompts people to buy a dozen. Most know this as the Decoy Effect, but there's more here at play. Eating off a dozen donuts is not easy, and this being a perishable item, people would have to share.

Now, let's talk about Carmine's restaurant in New York. You couldn't get a booking for just 2 people. You needed a minimum of 5, which means you'll tell others about it and get them along.

This is word of mouth by design, when you make your customers share your products or get others to try them with them - while you get paid for it too.

So the next time you think of sending a sample of your product, send 2 instead of 1 and get them to share it with someone who may need it.

69. 90-9-1 Rule for Online Communities

This is the 90-9-1 Rule for WhatsApp Groups and Online Communities.

Many individuals and groups are building an online community or even a WhatsApp group of people who are all committed towards the same cause. It could be to share knowledge on a subject, resolve study doubts, or discuss mutual interest areas such as soccer, street food, etc.

In all such groups, remember that 90% of the people will be just plain observers, who wouldn't participate.

9% will participate every now and then - probably give reactions when prompted.

And just 1% do all the heavy lifting of creating an impact.

This means if you're building a community that you would like to be forever engaged for a common cause, which could very well be for the purpose of serving your business, you should make peace with the fact that just 1% will do all the work.

And you would need 10 heavy lifters in the group to keep them engaged and growing.

70. Zero Party Data

Have you seen those YouTube polls recently on your smart TV?

Here's my guess on what they're about - Zero Party Data! Let me explain.

Internet browser cookies have enabled companies to track their customers' web activity and offer personalized product offerings, pricing, etc. for years. However, with governments, regulators and even consumers boycotting the collection of consumer data for commercial use against their will, or in fact, even without their knowledge, it has led to the emergence of a new method.

Companies are now finding ways for consumers to actively and knowingly give their own data to them in a gamified manner, which entertains the user, and offers specific insights on their preferences to businesses collecting them.

Unlike "third party data" which is passively collected by cookies, "zero party data" is actively collected through polls and quizzes.

The marketing campaigns designed on the basis of zero party data are known to show much higher conversion rates in sales than the earlier method of using data analytics on cookies.

Are you gamifying the collection of data on customer preferences in your business yet? If not, wait for a regulation to ban any other way of passively collecting this information, which will force you to build one such system.

I feel it's also a massive business opportunity for someone to build a tool to help businesses do this well.

71. Personal Brand for Business Success

Did you care as much about BoAt before you saw Aman Gupta on Shark Tank India?

I probably did a little bit knowing he's an alum of The Institute of Chartered Accountants of India as well as the Indian School of Business, so there was some commonality. Quite like students from my alma mater St. Columba's School, who cared way too much about Shah Rukh Khan because of the shared school.

Anyway, let's look at a few superstar entrepreneur names.

Elon Musk - Tesla, OpenAI, Hyperloop, SpaceX..

Varun Alagh & Ghazal Alagh - MamaEarth

Alakh Pandey - PhysicsWallah

Shantanu Deshpande - Bombay Shaving Company

Dharampal Gulati - MDH

These are all different industries, and entrepreneurs are known to different degrees for different reasons.

The point is, when I buy a Bombay Shaving Company product, the founder's (now recognized) face comes to mind. Almost like he sold it to me because he was talking about the process of building the product on his podcast. I think I now probably care a little more about his product than I care about Gillette.

Why? Because data shows:

- Millennials and Gen-Zs prefer to buy, and have higher conversions when the message from a business is from an individual than from a "we". "Humanizing" your business gives you higher sales conversions.
- While we often prefer to not interact with producers (e.g. we'd rather buy online than make a phone call), there are ways in which we can feel like we're interacting with another person - without the effort. In recent decades, consumers have been evolving away from caring about material possessions to valuing self-expression.

Thus, even if it may be grossly unfair to link the rise in the value of BoAt / MamaEarth / Sugar Cosmetics to the founders' appearance on Shark Tank (because it would undermine the years of hard work and grit that they've put in), I would assume building a personal brand helps immensely with opening doors more easily.

So, your business must have:

1. Business Brand; AND
2. Preferably an attached Personal Brand that aids in:

- Humanizing your business
- Building relatability with the target audience
- Opening doors for you (with investors, advisors, easier access)
- Reflecting thought leadership

We recommend founders build a strong Linkedin presence

and engage in PR activities as an essential hygiene aspect of raising funds for their startup. Because, fortunately or unfortunately, Finance is more about Marketing than it is about Finance itself.

72. Colour of the Year

Do you know what's the color of the year for 2023, and why is it important for business?

The Pantone Colour Institute analyzes trends across fashion, media, marketing, politics and culture to predict the most influential colors for the coming year. The color for 2023 is called Viva Magenta.

When Pantone announces the color, hundreds of brands take a cue and use the prescribed combinations to create products that could be fashionable in the coming year. If you're in the space of fashion, design and marketing, and you didn't know this, you need to up our game in trends and prediction analysis.

The colour of the year is supposed to be used for product design and marketing, and not for a branding redesign.

While Pantone does not release the entire methodology for its prediction, it is said that it does so with large data sets of historic and cyclical colour preferences in marketing and fashion to make this choice, which can end up saving the entire marketing community a great deal of time, effort and cost.

But...if everyone will be using the same colours, where is the differentiation?

That has to be in your execution, or consciously deciding on picking an opposite colour to stand out? As long as it's a conscious data-backed solution, you're using predictive analysis, which is great.

The following are a few examples of how some businesses could use this information:

- Makeup brands could launch items in this colour
- Nike AirJordans limited edition could be launched in Viva Magenta
- Canva could use it in its templates to attract people with ready-to-use popular designs
- Interior design companies can launch products in this colour catalogue

73. Yu-Kai Octalysis for Gamification

Let's look at how Zomato uses the Yu-Kai Octalysis to gamify your food-buying experience.

It's well established that building gamification in your product, whether it's a food delivery app, payment app, messaging app, social media app or even a traditional service business, is essential to psychologically appeal to your customers so that they engage with you more and thus increase transactions, habitual use and stickiness.

If you want a checklist on gamification, the Yu-Kai Octalysis comes as a ready framework. Let's analyse each of the 8 ways.

1. Epic Meaning through a Larger Objective:

A customer should believe that he is doing something greater than himself or is "chosen" to do something.

This works best in communities when people feel a sense of purpose in contributing to the benefit of a larger group like Wikipedia or a Discord group.

Zomato: "Tell people if buying from Kaku Da Dhaba is worth it, and review it for other customers!!"

2. Accomplishment Markers:

Build PBLs - points, badges, leaderboards - to give users a feeling of having completed a challenge and won an accolade at every step. Celebratory confetti on your phone screen?

Zomato:

"Your food is being prepared and on the way!! Woohoo!"

"OMG, you've unlocked the Hadippa Foodie Badge!"

3. Empowering Creativity:

Give users the choice to pick between different options and see the results of their choices soon as a feedback loop to either continue or change course.

Zomato:

"Would you want to add fries and coke and unlock a combo and save Rs 99?"

"Pick any out of the following promo codes to see how much you can save."

4. Ownership:

Owning virtual goods, or building one's own avatar gives the user a feeling of belongingness and ownership over the product.

Zomato: "Foodie Level 8 unlocked, Burp!!!"

5. Social Influence:

Invoke feelings such as mentorship, acceptance, social responses, companionship, as well as competition and envy.

Zomato: "Share your Annual Food Report with your friends on Instagram with one click."

6. Scarcity:

Drive of wanting something because you can't have it - such

as come back 2 hours later to get your reward - this makes users constantly think of going back or waiting eagerly.

Zomato: "Hurry, Haldiram's is shutting down for the day in 15 mins."

7. Unpredictability:

Run a lottery to give the user the chance to win something

Zomato: "Free Paneer Roll unlocked on purchase worth over Rs 2100."

8. Loss Avoidance:

It could be to avoid losing previous work, or to avoid admitting that everything you did up to this point was useless because you are now quitting.

74. Brands of the Richest

What brands do the richest Indians wear, and where do they invest their money?

Hurun India analyzes and publishes reports on how the richest around the world spend and invest their money. A recent report surveyed 350 Indian millionaires (personal wealth of over Rs. 7 crores) and 42 HNIs (personal wealth of over Rs 100 crores) to find the following insights.

- There are over 4.5 lakh households with a wealth of over Rs 7 crores. Mumbai tops the list (20k) followed by Delhi (17k) and Kolkata (10k).
- As for investments, most prefer real estate as the largest chunk of their investment, followed by stocks.
- Mercedes Benz is the most preferred car, followed by Range Rover and aspiration for Rolls Royce and Lamborghini.
- Taj is the most preferred hotel, followed by the Oberoi and Leela.
- Rolex is the most preferred watch brand followed by Cartier and Audemars Piguet. ~60% have over 4 luxury watches.
- Louis Vuitton is the most preferred luxury brand followed by Gucci and Burberry.

› Tanishq is the most trusted jeweller.

Most of this sounds pretty obvious, right? Here's the kicker

› Old Monk is the most preferred liquor.

You can check out the survey results in Hurun India Wealth Report 2021 and Hurun Indian Luxury Consumer Survey 2021.

Personally speaking, having those brands is one thing. Bearing all of them together would probably make you look like a peacock.

There are some super understated, mostly unheard of HNI luxury brands for the ones with old money. Because the super-rich don't buy brands, they buy bespoke.

Here's listing a few - Zilli, Kiton, Stefano Ricci, Brioni, Cesare Attolini, Loro Piana, Berluti, Charvet, Yves Salomon, Patek Philippe, Vacheron Constantin, Graff, Giambattista Valli.

Why do you need to know the understated ones? Understand your target customer persona, and learn their preferences and vocabulary like no one else does.

It probably varies with demographics such as age, generation, geography. And a degree of self-worth.

75. Red Bull Isn't a Beverage Company`

Red Bull is not a beverage company. Here is an insight not commonly known from its image.

Do you see how massive its marketing spend is compared to the top line when you compare it to other beverage leaders? However, there's more.

The company manufactures nothing. Its bottling is done by Raunch, an Austrian bottler. Also, the formula is not proprietary to RedBull like Coke is to Coca-Cola. No secret recipe that it owns!

The Founder, Mateschitz, is a marketing executive who discovered the drink in Thailand. But to make it look premium, he positioned it as an upscale beverage by making the can thinner and pricier than Coke.

Also, there's more to Red Bull owning an F1 team than what meets the eye. Through Red Bull's first 14 years in F1, the company invested $2.3B. Over the same period, Red Bull Racing is estimated to have created $300m+ a year in brand exposure, which is a total of over $5B+. That's a 2x return on investment and Red Bull owns the underlying asset. If Red Bull had spent on ads, that would've been just a one-time thing.

It's like performance marketing vs SEO. It's about ads for sales vs ads for brand building.

I'd say marketing and storytelling are the most important

functions of modern finance. No kidding. I did my specialization in Marketing at ISB after practicing as a CA for a few years.

76. Dimples on Golf Balls

Why do golf balls have dimples on them?

It's said that dimples on golf balls reduce drag, which means it goes farther with the same effort.

Now, let's imagine you've discovered this science, and you think it has more applications that could be pathbreaking if applied to other industries. Where else do you need to reduce drag? Airplanes? Cars? Let's start with cars!

In 2012, two gentlemen tested this premise on the TV show Mythbusters. Dimples were applied to a car by adding a layer of clay to the surface, which actually increased the car's weight significantly.

In their tests, the unmodified car gave 26 miles per gallon at a constant speed of 65 miles per hour. At the same speed, the dimpled car gave 29 miles per gallon, an 11.2% increase despite the increase in weight.

So would you put dimples on your entire car? Probably not because of two factors: the looks may not appeal to the customer, and the impact on the cost of manufacturing may drive up prices significantly.

The mileage is important to the consumer, but so are looks and the social factor the car brings.

This is probably the same reason why changing the shape of a few products may lead to lesser wastage in packaging and reduce logistics costs, but if it reduces the comfort of use of the product for the end customer, the cost saving through changing the shape is not what you want to do.

Not all projects that drive efficiency in business are equal. Not all problems are equal.

As the Marketing Professor at HBS, Theodore Levitt, puts it: "People don't want quarter-inch drills, they want quarter-inch holes." Marketers will justify better features in drills, and add frill after frill to the product to sell a "superior product" to the customer not realizing that those product improvements are irrelevant to the customer's needs.

77. Power Guarantee

Have you seen Ankur Warikoo claim that if you don't see value in his course, 100% of your money back?

Now it's easy for you to think that people selling online courses can say this because their cost of delivering one extra unit of sale is nothing, but that's where you're probably wrong.

This is called a "Power Guarantee", and it does something amazing for your sales.

Statistically, no more than ~5% of your customers will ask for their money back, but this very promise can triple your sales!

I have no idea about Ankur's numbers, but so many businesses offer money-back guarantees, and it works because:

- The consumer courts anyway have the power to ask you to return the money to a disgruntled customer. If you might have to do it under the law, why not make it a claim worth advertising?
- It builds credibility and pushes people to make the purchase right now instead of deferring it to later.
- It pushes the business to provide maximum value to the customer and thus requires you to perform better than the competition by design.

78. Negative Connotation in Communication

Remember to carry an umbrella.

While both of the above statements mean the same, which one would you use?

The second statement has a negation, i.e. using words like "don't", "never", "no", etc.

A recent study (July 2022) by a team that evaluated ~8k social media posts each across Facebook and Twitter, found that using negation in your communication increases engagement rates online by ~18% - and thus, all brands should try and frame their communication using negation to appear stronger or more powerful/authoritative.

It's an important insight for drafting B2C communication for your product online.

79. Fear vs. Humour

Do you still enjoy watching Andaaz Apna Apna? I used to be a big fan, but I now think it's pretty juvenile.

Also, tell me if you'll still be scared of the dark in a room that you've never been into before.

I was reading about RL Stine, the author of the children's horror book series, Goosebumps. The series has sold over 400 million copies worldwide and I'm sure you would've spotted them at the Scholastic Fair at your school back in the day.

Turns out that Stine used to author joke books before he switched to the horror genre. And switched because he soon realized that scaring people is easier than making them laugh.

And the more you think about it, the more you realize the truth.

You might find something funny, and your friend may not, but almost everyone is afraid of falling, of big reptiles, of losing a loved one, etc. Those fears almost never change with race, age, and gender across the world.

And then I think about how when businesses market themselves, ads and marketing collateral based on humor are more topical or short-lived than campaigns that run based on fear.

Your insurance companies continue to scare you about

losing a loved one, while a CRED or Bingo Mad Angles may be trying to use nostalgia once, a slapstick joke in another campaign, and then some other.

Jokes that I once guffawed at in the sitcom, The Office, I may now think are absolutely inappropriate. This probably indicates that when businesses want to run a campaign or branding to last several years on a channel that is traditional, they may try to evoke fear. And those who want to run campaigns that are shortlived on swiftly evolving channels, that would hopefully go viral for a very short span of time, would tend to do humour.

80. Earned Discounts

This is the marketing trick a car company used to sell a model that no one was ready to buy!

Most teams running performance marketing for companies recommend that you give more discount to boost sales. However, this is a terrible strategy because it reduces the "perceived value" of your product from premium to just one that is competing on price with several others.

As per consumer psychology, people value a discount much more when they have earned it. Let's look at a few cases where companies have been able to do this.

Renault wanted to get rid of its Dauphine model in the '60s, but even deep discounting wasn't selling the cars. They made a small nick in the paint of the car and said anyone who would spot it would get a $500 discount on the car. The cars were sold out in no time.

There are hundreds of apps that find ways to offer you discounts and rewards if you complete X number of steps in a month, or walk a total of Y km.

If you use the Cult.Fit app, you know how if someone joins Cult with your reference, you get 15 extra days in your membership.

Remember, people value the discount more if they put in some effort to obtain it, rather than it being provided for free. Further, when a buyer believes that they are close to earning a discount, they are more likely to buy more products or services to meet the required amount.

81. Listen to Sell Better

Have you ever had to undergo surgery? Or visit a doctor for an emergency, for yourself or a loved one?

Look back and think about which doctor made you feel most comfortable.

For most people, the number one quality in a doctor that signals confidence in their skill is not years of experience or how high up in the hospital's hierarchy they are, it is how patiently they sat and heard you explain your problem, with no rush, just actively listening to you describe your problem.

Those doctors consistently around the world get the highest ratings because they care to listen to the customer's problems.

While I would hate to equate the medical profession with business, I work as an advisor to hospitals and medical agencies, and it's these doctors who also get the highest requests for meetings with new patients, and make more money than the others. Not to say that they "listen" to patients only to get more conversions in business. But, more customers come to them because they listen, and that as a by-product, helps them make more money too.

The same thing applies to being a salesperson.

A salesperson's job is not to talk, but to listen. Just ask the right questions in an attempt to help the prospect find the right answer to their problem. A lot of times, the answer may not be the product that you're trying to sell, but a competitor's solution, or free advice on some hack to solve it (from prior experience).

And just that willingness to hear the prospect's pain points helps one have better conversions.

82. Content Creation Framework

How many videos does a creator need to make to get to 1 Million YouTube subscribers?

Tubebuddy is a YouTube analytics tool, which analyzed data of 3.5 Mn users in 2020 and published a report, which provided the following statistics.

The average number of videos for channels with:

› 1k-10k subscribers = 152

› 10k-100k subscribers = 418

› 100k - 1Mn subscribers = 1171

› 1Mn subscribers = 3873

So, going by averages, be ready to upload 3873 videos over the next few years.

Do remember that this data for YouTube is only from 2020. The pandemic post-March 2020 gave a moon-shot boom to creators, and platforms such as TikTok and Instagram made some overnight influencers.

But here are some insights that may be useful.

Only 2 of my videos went micro viral in the first 400 that I uploaded on Instagram and contributed to over 150k followers - that means a success rate of 0.5% virality for my niche, subject, and style of videos when I was creating and uploading daily.

Read "The Attention Factory", the story of TikTok and you'll learn that short-form video platforms make some creators stars overnight in an attempt to motivate thousands of others to create videos to invoke the feeling of "if they can, why can't I" - but this was the creator just plain getting lucky. Lucky because an actual person sitting somewhere pushed a heat button on their profile.

However, if you want to get lucky as a content creator, know that the output metric (no. of followers, subscribers, etc) is not in your control - you need to optimize for input metrics that are:

Consistency - do you have the motivation, grit, and perseverance to keep creating videos daily or weekly for an extraordinarily long period of time without caring too much about monetization?

Authenticity - The next thing to focus on is maintaining your voice and personality without blindly copying any other successful creator's style - because only authenticity will take you far.

Here is a breakdown of my content creation process. It is not over 20 mins a day, split into various activities:

- 5 mins of writing an insight down
- 5 mins of shooting
- 10 mins of upload across channels

Don't budget more than 30 mins a day if you want to do it consistently at first.

What is in it for businesses and startups? As a business know that content marketing is now one of the most efficient methods of community building and customer acquisition. Every business now needs a content creation function.

83. 3 Pricing Mantras

Three pricing mantras to never forget in your startup.

1. Freemium is an acquisition strategy, not a price point:

Giving your customers a freemium account helps you build a funnel and lead generation tool for paid users in the future. And when such freemium users convert to a paid plan, they end up showing a lower Customer Acquisition Cost, better Retention and better NPS metric (Net Promoter Score). However, if you count your freemium users as "customers", you are fooling yourself and your conscience (slash investors).

2. Larger Discounts lead to Larger Churn:

Try not to give a discount of more than 20% on your products or services, ever. While heavy discounts help you get more one-time users, the churn or the rate at which they leave is also massive, and most of the time leads to worsening your LTV to CAC ratios. Increase your perceived value proposition, not your discount. If you're having to discount a lot, you are probably in a highly competitive market, or people can't see the value proposition in your category-creating product.

3. Great Design & Social Proof can increase willingness to pay by over 35%:

It's said that a better-looking, premium design helps you get 20% more conversions, and case studies (deeper dives than testimonials) build social proof and credibility, which helps you charge 10-15% more.

84. 10-5-20 Rule of Pricing

There are primarily 4 levers to increasing profits: price, variable cost, volume and overheads. Out of these, the one that makes the highest impact with the least effort is increasing the price of your product.

Follow the 10-5-20 Rule in Pricing to check that you're not leaving money on the table.

- Justify 10x the value to your customer for the price that you charge - this could be perceived value as helping the customer get more revenue or reduce cost equivalent to 10x the price you've charged, where time saved is also cost reduction.
- Increase price by 5% till the time you lose no more than 20% of total paying customers - you might optimize your revenue at this price point. This 20% threshold is on the basis of Pareto principle.

Know that you want to try not to be in an industry that is extremely price sensitive and you cannot differentiate your product on quality or premium features. If it's a highly commoditized product, your chances of earning high profits only come with scale.

85. 10-Point Framework for 10x Price Rise

If you were forced to increase your prices by 10x, what would you have to do to justify it?

I read about this question on A Smart Bear blog, and it got me on a spiral of thinking of questions that every business owner/startup founder must ask themselves time and again. I say this because very few businesses would be in a place to get into a price war with competitors. The game is about how to charge higher prices for a higher value proposition. I borrow some of these from others and add a few of my own.

Here's a 10-point framework to think through:

1. Which brand in the market looks like a 10x price compared to you?
2. What will you change about your quality of service or product to match them?
3. What subset of the market will you target?
4. What kind of new and different problems will you have to solve for that market?
5. Will your high price look like a positive because they'll get a feeling of reduced risk due to better quality?
6. How will you allow them to share/showcase a badge of working with you as a "luxury" item?
7. How will your relationship be different with each cus-

tomer to justify this?

8. Can you seek 10x price by increasing cost by just 3x?
9. What kind of people would you need to hire to be like them?
10. How will your website and social media presence have to change to reflect a 10x proposition?

86. Profit or Cost?

Are you a Profit person or a Cost person at your organization? It determines your next promotion!

You'd have studied concepts of Profit Centres and Cost Centres. It's something that is discussed in Management Accounting and is a well-established part of the mid-modern business lingo.

Profit Centres are departments that bring in the money - sales and front-end customer-facing roles. This could be a Partner at a professional firm, a sales team for a SaaS company, and the like. Every other function is a cost centre, such as accounting, finance, data analytics, R&D, etc.

Now, not to say that support functions are not valued, but it should always be your objective to be perceived as a profit centre or someone who gets money in rather than money out. This helps you advance in your career, get more respect and better work opportunities.

Now you'll say that tech guys, despite being cost centres, are highly paid with huge upside in career opportunities. But know that their pay is a function of the demand and supply of that particular skill in the market. As and when the supply was being fulfilled from India, all the tech and service work was being outsourced to India.

Companies outsource cost centres to low-cost jurisdictions, but no one outsources their profit centres. To have an outside sales team is mostly unheard of, not to say that it doesn't exist.

And remember, you could very well be a profit centre despite being a tech worker or in finance. It's about how you're perceived in the organization.

Ways to evaluate yourself as a profit centre:

› How much money have you brought in increased sales through your work in the business?

› How much cost have you saved the company through your work?

› Are you sure no one else can deliver the same value as you do at a lower cost than you charge?

If you can't quantify the above yourself, you'll have trouble being perceived as a profit centre.

87. Engine as a Service!

Rolls Royce has the most unique pricing model for its airplane engines.

RR realized that airline companies want to be in the business of flying passengers from one point to the other, focusing on hospitality, economies, etc - and not on maintaining airplanes and their jet engines.

So they started a subscription business called "power-by-the-hour" by which they installed their engines in the airplane company's aircraft, and charged a price based on the number of hours the plane flew. It was Engine as a Service, with full maintenance of those engines.

RR handled installations, maintenance, upkeep, and switching of old engines for new ones, and this helped their customers convert a fixed cost to variable cost - thus reducing their upfront capital spend on buying planes with expensive engines.

I can imagine a similar model appearing in the EV space with Battery-as-a-Service (BaaS) and am glad the government is moving the needle in that direction too. Can be a massive, massive market!

That aside, are you building something to convert a fixed cost of your customers into a variable cost?

88. Audi's Pricing Play

Audi used this pricing principle to rival BMW and Mercedes for over 20 years.

Audi did not enjoy the same prestige as BMW or Merc in the 1980s and 90s. However, it stuck around and rivalled these players in prestige value as the 2000s arrived. There have been several strategic reasons, but there's a principle in pricing that they remembered.

If your industry has competitors that play on brand value, prestige and quality, and you're a new player, you should never reduce your prices to get market share. You should launch at a high enough price, and of course, you'll have fewer people ready to bet on a new entrant at that price.

In such markets, customers associate high prices with high quality and reduced prices with low quality or low prestige.

So, as a new brand, price your product at the value corresponding to your true quality, and you may have to patiently wait through time to a point when customers realise the price-value relationship.

Audi waited 20 years to get its brand to the price and prestige position it deserved.

If you have the choice to compete on price or quality, please choose quality even if it means lower sales initially. It's easy to reduce prices later but very difficult to increase prices.

89. Pricing Subscriptions Smartly

Imagine you have to pay a subscription charge of Rs. 12,000 for a year's access to a gaming website. It may seem like a ridiculously high amount, but what if they were to tell you that it costs less than your daily cup of coffee at just about Rs 30 per day?

It doesn't seem that bad after all.

So while communicating prices for subscription products, break it down into how cheap it is per day or per week or per seat or per user.

But, charge it upfront at once. Because if you bill at a monthly interval, maybe the person may feel they're not using it as much and would decide to not renew after a couple of months.

Gyms do this all the time.

Remember, anchor your price as a per-day cost, but charge for the year upfront.

90. Pricing model for SaaS companies: Freemium or Free Trial?

Which pricing model works better for SaaS companies: Freemium or Free Trial?

Freemium puts a price on functionality that means, few features are free to use, and for advanced features, you pay money.

Free Trial puts a price on time of use, i.e. all features free for some time and then you pay to use it all.

Freeimum works better when:

- User value is dependent on network effects
- User adoption is dependent on virality (word of mouth marketing)
- Users have low willingness to pay
- Functionality demanded by business users is different from that of free individual users

Free trial works better when:

- Users are assigned and created by an admin
- Utility to paid users is not diminished if free users fall off
- The utility is targeted to people with relatively higher willingness to pay
- Time-based paywall creates urgency which helps expedite the sale

91. Soaps, Cigarettes, and the Union Budget

Why would retailers sell Lifebuoy and Lux at a loss every February?

Every year, India's major FMCG players would see that shopkeepers would end up selling huge quantities of soap at a loss in February. This was against the company's pricing policies and rules and they wanted to dig deeper to find out the motivations.

The shopkeepers would get a 30-day credit from the FMCG distributors. Every Feb, they would sell the stock quickly at a loss and use the money collected from customers to stock ITC cigarettes.

This was because it was expected that at the soon-to-be-announced Union Budget, the govt would increase taxes on cigarettes and the prices will go up.

The shopkeepers would use the money collected from soaps to buy cigarettes, which would sell at a higher price the following month. The profits made on those cigarettes would offset the losses on the sale of soap.

Indian businessmen are really smart when it comes to thinking of using credit and managing working capital to profit their business. Are modern-day startups doing the same?

92. High Velocity for Low Margins

What to do in business when you don't have a high-margin product?

If you don't have high margins, you need scale. But what can you do in the interim when you don't yet have scale?

You go for high velocity, i.e. rotate your stock as soon as possible, or swift stock turnover

Attempt to do the following as fast as you can:

› Get payments for your products upfront (no later than 15 days)

› Make payments to your vendors in 45 days (max allowable limit under MSME act)

› Keep inventory or stock for not over 15 days

I know a bunch of these things may seem intimidating in your industry at first, but velocity trumps margins. If you don't have margins, you MUST aim for velocity.

93. The Art Valuation Scam

80% of art sales by value are within the countries of USA, UK and China. And 50% of the total sales value is carried by just the top 1% art that is traded.

While theoretically and to the open world, art valuation is a function of:

› Size: directly correlated

› Genre: minimalism, portraits, modern art

› Authenticity: density of paint, cracks, color fade, signature

› Place: Museums and galleries where it has been exhibited; and most importantly

› Reputation: of the artist, the dealer, and the intended purchaser.

The last part of the above list is where lies the entire game of valuation.

Art galleries maintain huge opacity in prices and it's essentially a price-fixing scheme between collectors and galleries, the intermediaries who keep changing the prices depending on who the buyer is. They decide who to sell to so that they can increase their prestige value and command a higher price for all their other paintings.

As for buyers, they may keep bidding higher prices for

paintings because they may own other paintings by the same artist and may want the value of their collection to go up.

Internationally, the "rich" also use it to launder cash money or evade taxes by donating art at inflated notional prices to galleries across the world. And using the donation tax breaks as per their tax jurisdictions.

94. Avoid Deal Seekers

Which type of customer should you avoid as much as possible?

It's the deal seekers!

When online businesses feel that they're not growing fast enough or are not getting as many downloads or registrations as they used to, they make the suicidal mistake of going after deal seekers, giving huge discounts on their offerings to get more users.

They think having more users will help build the right traction numbers for the next round of valuation and getting to a million users will be a wonderful milestone that will elevate them to the next league.

This will increase the CAC for now, but they'll extract LTV later. They remind themselves of the Gillette model, where razors are inexpensive but blades are expensive, or the printer and ink model.

However, what they fail to do is build a product that is so sticky that a customer will not be able to move out of the ecosystem easily because it's habit forming.

So if you build a non-habit-forming product, and give huge discounts to get users (deal seekers), you've committed harakiri, because beyond a particular threshold, it's the user retention or activity that drives business value.

And as the deal seekers come only for the discount, and

have no loyalty to the product, it drops the overall repeatability ratio of the product, and in fact, shows the company poorly in comparison to the competition.

The LTV never comes in, and the CAC is already incurred and wasted. There is no payback!

So in most cases, avoid falling prey to the urge of reducing prices to get more users. Deal seekers do not make repeat purchases, as they have no loyalty.

Building a habit-forming product is much harder than giving away deals. In most cases, the combination may lead to huge financial losses and a decrease in business valuation.

95. Limited Edition Pricing Mistake

This is the pricing mistake a luxury watch company made.

Baselworld is one of the largest watch fairs in the world and has the grandest luxury watch brands showcasing their new models to the public.

One of the well-known watch companies had an extremely popular watch that used to sell for about Rs. 16 lakhs. So at the following Baselworld, they launched a new model of that watch with a 50% price increase, somewhere around Rs. 24 lakhs, and because the price was steep, they limited it to only 1000 pieces.

As it turned out, they received orders for 3.5k pieces at that high price. Now this being publicly announced limited edition, they could not release more units - but this shows how much money was left on the table.

Had they sold the watch for 30L instead of 24L, and sold just 1000, they would've made 60 crores more in profits!

For anyone running a simple D2C brand who faces stock out of a popular item in your inventory, rather than just solving the problem of ordering enough inventory for next month, you must explore increasing prices of that product and not leaving money on the table. It's a direct signal to increase prices, in most cases.

96. OBPPC Pricing

Coke in a can costs about Rs 13/100 ml and in a 250 ml bottle, it's approximately Rs 8/100 ml. So Coke in a can is almost 60% more expensive. If you take a 2L bottle, it may cost lesser than Rs 3/100 ml. Let's understand why Coke uses differential pricing using the OBPPC framework.

You may still find a 2L Coke bottle and a 300 ml can together at a grocery shop, but almost never the 250 ml bottle with a 300 ml can.

There is a clear strategy of customer segmentation at play here with an attempt to maximize profits. To put it simply, cans are for single-use consumers at premium locations such as airports, movie theatres, and malls, while bottles are a market penetration product attempting to capture customers in price-sensitive areas. This is how Coke attempts to capture customers both in Gurgaon and Ballabhgadh.

This is a clever implementation of the OBPPC (Occasion-Based Pricing and Promotion for Consumer Goods) framework!

Occasion: Coca-Cola strategically identifies two main consumption occasions: single-use (think quick snack breaks) and shared consumption (family meals, social gatherings).

Price Sensitivity: Coke knows that single-use can customers are willing to pay a premium, while pet bottle customers are more price-sensitive.

Promotion: Coke tailors promotional strategies to target customer segments and consumption occasions effectively. They show bottles in Diwali ads because family-based celebrations are always in groups and more about sharing things. While in ads based on sporting events, they always highlight the actor drinking out of a can.

Also, Coke cans at airports are longer, have you noticed?

It's also because they need a reason to charge a higher MRP at the airport for the merchants to stock them and recover higher operating costs. Being able to identify occasions and the associated price sensitivity is key to implementing this framework well. And if you can market your products using this differentiation as well, you are bound to make good returns.

97. Dynamic pricing

Coca-Cola once changed its prices with the ambient temperature.

Back in 1999, Coca-Cola tried a dynamic pricing model in Japan, where they coded vending machines to increase prices when the outside temperature rose. It was done with the help of a thermometer attached to the machine. Consumers soon realized what Coca-Cola was up to and it led to quite a consumer outrage where the beverage manufacturer eventually switched to static prices.

In modern times, dynamic pricing is also prevalent in airline ticket booking and hotel booking. Based on your past online purchases and browsing history, and also based on how close to the actual date of interest you are booking the flight/hotel you would have to pay a premium.

People often talk about finding investment opportunities that beat inflation to preserve the purchasing power of their money and make it grow, but an alternative approach could be to increase prices in your business to beat inflation.

If you run a business, consider increasing your prices by at least 7%, in line with consumer inflation currently. If you don't consider an efficient price increase or cost reduction of an equivalent amount, you would have to bear the brunt of thinning profits. The FMCG industry often moves prices north to account for inflation rates.

Part 4
Startup Notes: Things Startups Go Through

Being a founder of a startup and making it successful is one of the hardest things for any professional to accomplish. And since I work with so many of them, I know now that it's impossible to predict every challenge that can arise. Nonetheless, everyone can still consume wisdom from people and resources around and give themselves the best chance to succeed.

In this section, I have collated some interesting insights about building a startup without going into the details. The topics range across idea generation, market size, product building, marketing, and a few other fascinating theories. Treat this section like my collection of startup notes which most founders and leaders wouldn't have come across elsewhere. While my last book, *Daily Coffee & Startup Fundraising*, helped you understand startups and fundraising in detail, this section is like the revision notes that keep you afloat and stimulated.

Note that neither can be interchanged with the other, and whether or not you have read my first book, you will find value here regardless.

98. What to Build?

If you want to start up and are unsure of what to build, here is a guiding framework that can help.

Your first point of consideration should be the network or the platform.

The second should be SaaS or Software.

Finally a direct-to-consumer(D2C) model.

Let's understand the framework in detail.

The barrier to entry for starting a D2C brand is very low. You set up an online store, maybe on Shopify, get products contract manufactured, start running ads and content on social media to establish an online presence and boost sales, and also sell through platforms like Amazon. If you're starting a D2C brand today, know that every brand is competing with another. There is no brand loyalty among those who can afford to pay for your product in India. Customer Acquisition Cost (CAC) and marketplace commissions are ruthless and eat up your entire margin and more.

The time for setting up a D2C brand was probably 2016-18. Since then people have milked it, burnt money in building a brand, and have moved on. To start another one today is excruciatingly hard unless you own the manufacturing or a distribution platform as a massive creator/influencer.

This brings us to the first consideration. Building a platform with network effects is much harder in comparison, but way more beneficial in the long run with immense wealth generation potential. Zomato, Amazon, and Google; all of them eat up your margin whether the businesses listed on them make money or not. Find a market that is unorganized and focus on organizing it. That's where a moat will lie. It's much harder than starting a D2C brand, but this is where a massive wealth generation kingdom is actually made.

If you understand tech and can get a team to build software to automate a process which is currently manual, building SaaS or enterprise software is the way to go.

Between the two, I personally prefer Enterprise because B2B sales may be easier if you can get meetings and your product genuinely adds value. For consumer SaaS products like Spotify, you might need crazy marketing spends again to acquire users.

Software is better because once you acquire a customer who loves your product and is locked in on using it, it leads to amazing LTV to CAC ratios which are indicative of robust businesses.

So remember,

First comes network or platform.

Second comes SaaS or Software.

Last comes D2C.

99. Find Your Idea

When you identify a problem which needs to be addressed, figuring out a possible solution leads to the birth of a startup idea. Often it feels exhilarating in the beginning but how do you decide if it is right for you?

There are several frameworks to evaluate the feasibility of a business idea and whether it's worth pursuing; and it's even better if the idea creates an impact and makes you some wealth.

However, to know if that idea or effort is right for you as a personality, you should use the POS Framework, where POS stands for:

› Passion

› Opportunity

› Skillset

If you have the *passion* for something and there's a huge *market opportunity* for it, but unfortunately you do not have complementary *skills*, you'll probably fail.

If you have the *skill* and there's an *opportunity*, but no *passion*, you might make money, but with drudgery. How long can you keep working on something which you are not passionate about? Eventually, the energy will fizzle out.

If you have the *passion* and the *skill*, but there's not a big enough *opportunity*, then you'll have fun while working on it, but will probably not end up making a lot of money.

This framework has been recommended by Avnish Bajaj of Matrix Partners India, and seems to have been inspired by the concept of Ikigai.

100. Entrepreneurial Traits

Founders flock to investors in hordes to raise capital. Some have a brilliant nascent idea, some have a functioning MVP, and some could also have strong traction in the market. It becomes important for investors to have a framework to identify people or ideas which would be successful in the long run. Startup investors, just like retail stock investors, would never want to bet on a company that is less likely to make money. So, how do they decide who to back?

It turns out that a combination of the idea and the people executing the idea is bet upon. Often the people executing the idea take precedence. In such cases, it becomes important to understand how investors evaluate founders and the skills they look for.

This framework used by Matrix Partners evaluates entrepreneurs to see if they have what it takes to succeed. The following traits are judged on a scale of 0, 0.5, and 1.

1. Curiosity
2. Grit
3. Hunger
4. Self Control
5. Zest

6. Social Intelligence
7. Optimism
8. Gratitude
9. Hustle

You could rate yourself and your co-founders on these traits. In general, a score of over 6 and above is considered great. Be careful of the confirmation bias which can creep in if you rate each other as founders on this framework.

101. How Many Co-founders?

With an ever-increasing focus on startups, and many fresh ideas being worked upon, an obvious question is how many people should be co-founders in a startup? What is the Optimal number? 1, 2, 4? Let's find out.

TechCrunch reviewed over 7k companies on Crunchbase that raised over USD 10 Mn and found the average number of founders for them to be 1.85. Just 22% of the companies had 3 or more founders, and almost 46% had just one founder.

There are enough data sets which will give you the average number of founders being close to 2, and it of course helps to have 2 co-founders. But half of those companies were also created by solo founders. Obviously, there is no one rule which fits all.

One could debate the qualification of the startups captured under this tenet of having raised 10 Mn or more from investors, and the bias of such an approach. I personally do not think raising 10 Mn or more is a standard for success for any business but this study is backed by data and the results are in your favour if you are a solo founder or a pair of two.

Remember this is just an indicative study and by no means mandates limiting the number of co-founders in a startup to two. There are plenty of success stories with three or more co-founders.

102. Resolving Conflicts

Co-founder conflict is the biggest reason for startup failures. Working in an environment with multiple unknowns and varied personalities often leads to disagreements in opinions and thoughts. Just shooting down your partner's new idea or aggressively debating it may not be the most ideal way to deal with it.

In a lot of cases, people maintain a firm stand on what according to them is the best course of action, and they might be looking for external validation than genuine advice on whether an idea should be pursued or not. If you debate or deny, chances are they may still go ahead and execute.

One way of dealing with this situation could be to come to a middle path. Agree with them on short-term milestones to be achieved for the new idea, milestones which should be met successfully within the coming weeks or months. Post this evaluation period it is mutually decided if the idea would be pursued further or dropped. This methodology works due to two factors. Due to prior agreement of specific milestones, founders have a clear vision of expectations from the idea or initiative. Once the agreed time frame has passed you have proper data to evaluate the success or failure of the initiative. Irrespective of whose idea it was, with clear expectations and actual data to back further decision-making, most fallouts can be prevented.

103. The VC Investment Funnel

If you have been building your own startup for a while and have reached a stage of maturity in terms of product development and early traction, chances are you would be talking to investors and VCs soon enough. It is important to understand the VC investment funnel so that you are prepared for what is to come.

For every 100 deals that a Venture Capital firm would want to evaluate for investment, they decide to meet founders of just 28.

These 28 firms get to meet with an Analyst or Associate, usually a junior person who is supposed to weed out the possibilities further by studying the market the startups operate in, the opportunity, and the overall business model. Just 10 out of these 28 go up to the Partners for serious consideration.

Out of those 10, only 5 may go to the next stage of deeper due diligence, and finally, 1 may get a term sheet and a deal closure.

This means even when you have secured a meeting with a fund, there is a small 3.5% chance of that converting to a term sheet.

The idea here is not to dissuade you, but to make you aware of the reality. Do not lose hope if you've done 20 meetings and none of them converted.

It takes a lot of hustle. A lot of it.

Also, warm intros to funds have a 16 times higher chance of closure than cold emails.

P.S. Amazing stats I read in Sajith Pai's summary of the book, The Unicorn's Shadow by Ethan Mollick.

104. Founder Salaries

Depending on what stage your startup is in, your ability to negotiate for your salary changes. Below are a few benchmarks that are prevalent in the industry and can be used to decide on your own salaries.

- **Seed:** Most founder salaries at the seed stage are just enough to manage their basic personal expenses. Salaries are usually in the range of Rs. 1-1.5 lakhs per month depending on the city you're living in and the amount of funding the startup has raised. Ideally, no more than 10% of the total funding amount should go into the hands of the founders if the funding is less than Rs 2 crores.
- **Series A:** At this point, you should negotiate with investors to double the salary payout to a monthly in-hand amount, which is at par with the talent the startup has to hire immediately on closing Series A.
- **Series B:** Negotiate a secondary sale of some shareholding to incoming investors so as to generate some cash in hand which can be used for building assets and savings. This is the first opportunity for the founder to cash out on their work and effort.

These are just indicative ideas to build on. Actual facts and reasonability of salaries and founder payouts may vary with industry, size of the fundraise, and need of the business.

105. Founder's Target Equity Ownership

How much equity should founders reserve for themselves?

Let's check out a few popular personalities and how much equity they hold for the companies they built.

(Note that these numbers are from mid-2022)

- Jeff Bezos holds ~11% of Amazon
- Mark Zuckerberg has ~13% of Meta
- Vijay Shekhar Sharma holds ~14.5% of Paytm
- Ritesh Agarwal holds ~7% of Oyo
- Deepinder Goyal holds ~5.5% of Zomato
- Falguni Nayar holds ~52% of Nykaa
- The 5 founders of Delhivery collectively own ~6-7%

While the above examples show a wide range of holdings from 5% to 50% of the company at a late stage close to IPO, these have the following learnings for founders while thinking of dilution.

Imagine you'll reach IPO in 10 years, and each time you raise money, it gives you 24 months of runway. You will need to reserve a minimum of 15% for ESOPs, advisors, the founding team, and CXOs.

You'll give away an average of approximately 17.5% in each

fundraising round which means roughly 70% of your company would be diluted in 4 rounds. The remaining 15% should be your minimum target ownership at IPO as a principle.

The more the number of founders, the target ownership gets split among them all leading to smaller individual holding, so they may target a higher collective ownership in such cases.

Note that this is just a framework and does not always hold true, but it gives you an idea about how to plan for dilution in future rounds of funding.

106. "Negative Controls" and "Positive Controls"

Once you have raised funds for your startup, and investors enter the fray, there are specific "controls" that you need to be aware of. Investor Controls are of two kinds, "Negative Controls" and "Positive Controls".

- Positive Control is the investor's ability to vote as a Director, which is fairly limited. It would also mean that the rights they have as shareholders are only meaningful if they have a controlling stake of 51% or more, which is typically not the case.
- Hence, instead of worrying about whether you should give your investor a Board seat or not, you should read, understand and strongly negotiate on the Negative Controls. "Negative Controls" means your business can't do certain things unless you get approval from your investors. These are also known as protective provisions, for example, future fundraising, change in shareholding structure, taking debt, merger or acquisition decisions, etc.

What you cannot negotiate to get removed, insist on getting a threshold in at the very least. For example, if a change in related party transactions would require investor approval, you should negotiate for the increase in related party transactions such that transactions beyond Rs. 50L per annum only would require investor approval.

107. TAM in India

Most Indian startups incorrectly size the markets they are going to operate in. Consider the following points.

- India has 140 crore people, out of which approximately 40 crore have mobile internet
- Out of these 40 crore people, only ~10 crore people regularly transact on UPI
- ~7 crore Indians are buying things online, and close to ~3 crore are not buying repeatedly
- Only ~3 crore people hold investments in stocks and Mutual Funds of over Rs 10k
- Less than ~1.5 crore people earn over Rs. 5L p.a.
- Zomato's monthly transacting users have plateaued at ~1.5 crore people for almost a year
- Less than ~75 lakh people contribute to over half of all online purchases from Amazon/Flipkart
- There are no more than ~50L households in India with an annual household income of >25L p.a.
- Less than ~10 crore people earn more than Rs. 20k per month
- If you're building an internet-based offering for a pre-

mium customer, your total market size in India is at a maximum of 75L people - something that Cred, Amazon Prime, and Netflix are already going after

Know that India has seen unprecedented growth in Internet users over the past 5 years because of cheaper internet access through Jio, cheaper smartphone accessibility through Chinese brands, and startups spending money to acquire new customers.

As most of these things are now beginning to plateau, similar growth rates may not be seen as much in the Total Addressable Market in the above segments, but only for companies that can go deeper into Bharat for lower priced products - essentially creating something of value for those who earn less than Rs. 20k per month, and may possibly be the only earning member of a household of 5.

When a country's economy grows, every player in the industry grows with it, but when economic growth plateaus, the only way for businesses to grow is to eat each other's market share. When this happens only the fittest and the fiercest survive.

P.S. The above data has been collected from the analysis and research of some brilliant teams and minds such as Praveen Gopal Krishnan of The Ken, reports from Zerodha and Nitin Kamath, as well as thoughts from the folks at The Indian Dream - Sahil & Siddharth. All these points were collected in mid to late 2022.

108. The iPhone Proxy

Do you know how many people in India use an iPhone? Almost 60 lakh iPhones were shipped to India in 2021, and about 70 lakh in 2022.

The iPhone user count in India is expected to cross 2 crores in 2023, making Apple's share ~5% of the smartphone market in the country. The highest number of iPhone users are in Delhi (18%), followed by Bangalore and Mumbai at 10-11% in each.

Approximately 70% of iPhones are bought on EMI - which means the surge in sales is happening because of BNPL(Buy Now Pay Later) and EMI financing schemes.

The flagship iPhone 14 Pro sells for Rs 1.3L, which is the average per capita income of Indians. The same phone costs about Rs. 82k in the US. The additional cost is on account of tax items such as GST and Customs Duty. Apple's revenue in India was over Rs. 33,000 crores in FY 2021-22, which was up 45% from the previous year. In comparison, Apple's global revenue only grew by 8% in the same period.

Retail stores earn a gross margin of 5-7% on an iPhone sale, which finally ends up at about 2-3% net margin. Online stores offer the product for about Rs 5k cheaper while maintaining the same margin.

Why is this data relevant? Most startups focus on a premium customer base or define Apple users as a proxy.

109. The 1-10-100 Rule

This small guideline helps startups find Product Market Fit and get on the treadmill for sustainable growth after the launch of their product. I call it the 1-10-100 rule.

› 1 Fanatic Customer Persona

We start with a well-defined persona. Who is the exact ideal person who would be an absolute fan of your product, and go nuts about the solution you offer because it actually gives them 10x value? Write down their exact description. Their age, where they live, how much they earn, what brands they love, where they hang out, what car they drive, what activities they do over the weekend, etc. Go into as much detail as possible.

› 10 Core Customers

You just list and shortlist those 10 core people who fit the customer persona, and you ensure that you're obsessed with keeping them engaged as they are the most likely to talk about your solution to others and start off a cycle of word-of-mouth marketing.

› 100 next Customers through the most efficient distribution channel

Evaluate if your product will reach a wider audience digitally or offline. Will they be at bookstores, airports, cafes, parks, or athletic meets? Then just go after that channel obsessively to onboard the next 100.

Once you have 100 people, you have enough data to find their churn rates, referral rates, engagement rates, etc., and that gives you insight into building your revenue model and growth plan with actual pilot data.

110. Flintstoning

A lot of us loved The Flintstones back in the day. It was a funny cartoon that imagined humans living with dinosaurs in pre-historic times. There's a lesson in it for product development.

Wilma, Dino, and the kids would be driven around by the man of the house, Fred, in a car which required him to run with his legs on the ground. What use was the car then?

A lot of times in tech and software product development, founders spend huge amounts of time and money building one feature after the other - but what matters more in a startup is to build a minimum viable product (MVP) and test it rapidly with users.

"Flintstoning" is typically referred to as the act of manually executing a customer request on a tech product because it has not been automated yet. For example, if the customer clicks on "cancel order", the order is canceled at the back-end by a person manually.

Flintstoning is important because it gives you time and cost efficiency to only build features that a lot of customers are utilizing on the app. At the beginning of your startup journey, if you have to put in manual efforts till the time you raise capital, go ahead and sweat it out, at least you will prioritize features based on customer feedback, utility, and data and not make decisions going by your gut.

111. The DDLJ Product Test

Run the DDLJ test on your startup.

What is the most functional (non-emotional) aspect of the movie that led to Raj and Simran finding love together?

A young man and a woman went on a Euro trip at the same time and ran into each other.

Now, this one action (function) led to other things like them falling in love, Raj winning over Simran's family, fighting with the other guy's sidekicks, and finally getting to *"jee le apni zindagi"*. Do you see how all the emotional outcomes are a result of some pre-requisite core functional actions? Going on a Euro Trip, bumping into an attractive person, and finding yourself in situations that would lead to love.

A lot of startups hear brand messages like - "Sell an emotion, not a function." Learn from Nike's "Just Do It" or Apple's "status appeal". What they forget is all these emotions are built only after solving for some core differentiating functions, which are clearly communicated to elite early adopters such as athletes (in the case of Nike) and tech+design aficionados in the case of Apple.

A lot of startups, D2C brands especially, tend to only be focused on the emotion lens, with barely any functional differentiator to begin with. Which will probably not build deep loyalties with their customer base.

The early parts of building a product are about solving core functional problems better than your competitors and getting validation from a narrow set of super-interested users.

Once it's established that your product is superior, then add emotion and status to market it to a broader audience.

I'll take the example of Ultrahuman. I feel they solved for the constant tracking of sugar spikes in your body on a phone app and then topped it up with a physical patch that brings you status by the fact that you're wearing it on your tricep with a short-sleeved t-shirt and good muscles to flaunt.

Trying to build emotion with no differentiated superior functionality, in most cases, is just superfluous spending on marketing in an over-competitive and commoditized market.

112. The Hard Side

If you work on a product that has two sides - suppliers and buyers, creators and consumers, drivers and riders, writers and readers - there is one side which has to do a lot more work to add value to the other. The suppliers, the drivers, creators, the writers - and this is the Hard Side.

When Tinder analyzed online dating trends, they figured that men swipe right on 45% of the women they see, but women only swipe on 5% of the men. This means women were the harder side to please and keep on the platform - and seemingly "more" and "better" women drove the success of an online dating app.

For anyone building a network effect in a product with two sides, they need to find ways to build incentives for the hard side to keep them retained and engaged on the platform.

In dating apps, this has been done through: giving them the first right to initiate messaging, building in-app messaging so that numbers don't have to be given out, connecting with Facebook to see mutual friends to build trust.

The hard side in your product has to be incentivized by any of the following:

- Monetizing their free time and resources
- Giving them higher social status, i.e. helping them find more ways to generate money or popularity (brand)

- Making things easier and faster for them

For most service companies, the hard side could be employees, countered by clients on the other side.

113. Metcalfe's Law

While a lot of people talk about building "network effects" in business, not much is spoken about how to put a financial value to the number of people in a network.

Network effects apply to technology products and businesses, where the utility of the product increases as more people start using the product, for example, Facebook, Uber, Slack, WhatsApp, etc.

A simple arithmetic method used in financial models takes a percentage of total users as paying users, and the amount that percentage pays over a period of time becomes a financial value. That is how you value a subscription business or any other linear business even with no network effects.

To prescribe a value to the "utility" increasing of the product such as having now your entire friend circle on WhatsApp, you have to study Metcalfe's Law - this increase in utility is in the form of more time spent, more stickiness, increased frequency of use, and high switching costs.

This law states that a network's value is proportional to the square of the number of users. So, by increasing the user base from 10 to 11 increases the user count by 10%, but increases the value of the network by 21% as it goes up from 100 to 121!

114. India 1, India 2 and India 3

If you are planning to build an Indian Startup, you must know this - India is divided into India 1, India 2 & India 3.

India 1 Alpha

This group consists of around 60L people who come from the top 5% of Tier 1 cities or the top 0.1% of Tier 2 Cities. They are an English-speaking crowd who are Westernized, and frequently travel by air, nationally or internationally. Most of these people come from cities like Mumbai, Gurgaon, Bangalore, and Pune. As it is one of the most affluent personas there are quite a few startups targeting them, such as Milkbasket, Cred, Netflix, Raw, LBB, etc.

India 1

India 1 consists of ~11 Crore people with a combined GDP of ~$1 Trillion GDP. They are fluent in English, digitally savvy, understand Western culture, and prefer convenience over cost. They hail from cities like Delhi, Mumbai, Kolkata, Chennai, Jaipur, and Goa. Companies like Dunzo, Uber and Oyo target this user group.

India 2

10.5 Crore people comprise the India 2 group and have a combined GDP of $300 Billion. They are vernacular speaking and aspire for a better life, but are not digitally very fluent. They mostly come from Tier 2 cities like Indore,

Lucknow, and Agra. Facebook, RailYatri, Meesho and ShareChat are trying to focus on this user base.

India 3

The lowest rung of the ladder in terms of digital fluency and education, this group is the most populous with ~112 Crore people within it. A whopping combined GDP worth $1.3 Trillion is attached to them. They hail from rural areas and Tier 3 cities. They are less educated, barely digitally capable, engaged in manual labor, and excited by content offerings. They are the target group for apps like WhatsApp and Youtube.

Every startup building in India must know of this classification in order to have correct estimates of

› Market Size

› Target Customer Persona

› Estimated Willingness of Customer to pay for offerings

While this concept is much talked about across mediums, it has been explained beautifully by Sajith Pai from Blume Ventures in their Indus Valley Annual Report 2022.

115. Scale of Tier 2, Tier 3 Indian Market

A lot has been spoken about targeting the right user base using products that resonate with them. A lot of companies in India focus on the Alpha group of the Indian diaspora, the richest 1% or even less, which is an extremely crowded space for D2C brands. The real scale is available beyond this group in tier 2, tier 3 cities. This is well known but few are able to capture the market as well as Campus, the footwear brand.

They are the largest sports footwear brand in India by revenue. It clocked Rs 1200 crores for FY 22 - that's a massive growth over the previous FY's 700 crores. Its market cap is USD ~2 Bn and it's been able to do this in just about 17 years.

While other international sneaker brands sell shoes upwards of Rs. 3500, Campus has captured a huge piece of the market for sneakers between Rs 500 to 1500.

You would wonder if Bata is a competitor too, but know that Bata has just about 500 SKUs in sneakers, while Campus has over 6000. That's more than even Nike in India.

India 1 Alpha has online spenders with high disposable incomes but are just about 75 lakh in the country, and a huge market is offline for the price-sensitive Tier 2, Tier 3 consumer.

116. Build For Everyone?

When TaxiForSure first launched, they used to get about 8 rides per day. But one day, data revealed that a customer had taken 59 rides in the last month.

On digging deeper they found out that it was a pregnant lady who would make frequent trips to the doctor, to yoga classes, and to breathing classes. She also had a strong feeling of community with other pregnant women for a prolonged period of 6-7 months.

In true startup hustle fashion, the founders soon started visiting maternity hospitals at 6 every morning and started telling pregnant women that they had built the best taxi service for pregnant women. They spoke to the target group first-hand and gathered all their requirements and considerations. They found out the women were concerned about the driver not being rash while handling the car, not honking, keeping the AC on, not playing music, among others. They built all those requirements as part of the SOP to serve these customers better.

Soon these women started using the taxi excessively and also told their friends, and the news spread across the entire community. Almost overnight, the company moved from 8 rides a day to 45.

As they say, when you enter a market, care about not getting a million customers who think you're decently okay, but instead get 100 who love you and obsess about you and can't stop talking about you. Gradually do add more user personas, but be careful about building for everyone.

Remember that when you build for all, you build for absolutely no one.

117. Lightbulbs Were a Startup

Thomas Edison invented incandescent electric light in 1879. The biggest hurdle to the bulb's adoption was the lack of commercially available electricity. For consumers to buy it seemed infeasible but Edison was relentless and enterprising.

Edison opened the USA's first commercial power plant within the next 3 years called Pearl Street Station - where it started serving 400 lamps to 82 customers. Within 2 years, they had started serving 10k+ lamps to 500+ customers.

Not just that, he also had to convince the government to dig up streets so that power distribution cables could be laid. That's a prime example of capitalist lobbying for the benefit of his commercial interest.

As electricity consumption measuring meters were not fully tested and validated, he did not bother sending any electricity bills to customers till 1883 and bore the cost of consumption. All of this is very relatable to anyone building a new tech startup today.

This approach seems impractical because how can you change the world to adopt your invention? It's a lot of hard work, conviction, perseverance, lobbying, and also bearing the initial cost of adoption.

So startup winter or not, just focus on creating value. The world shall follow.

118. The Turnaround Decision

Climbing down Mount Everest is 8 times more dangerous than climbing up.

Apart from requiring immense mountaineering experience and peak physical fitness, other factors that are strategized upon are the oxygen-carrying capacity in the tanks, speed of the climb, weather, and the time of the day so that there's enough sunlight.

Considering all of the above, "1 pm" in the afternoon is an established "turnaround time" - the time at which they have to descend the mountain so that they have enough sunlight on the way down, and can also ration their oxygen well enough to make it back in time, and not die of darkness or fatigue.

Similarly, there are several time-based milestones in the journey to scale Everest, which if you as a climber are unable to meet, you are required to go back and try again later.

These milestones and limits are similar to the concept of "stop loss" in stock trading. It is about defining a limit to which you're willing to go - beyond which you will take the tough decision of stepping back. This "stop loss" or "turnaround time" is an essential metric, which should be discussed in the context of startups as much as terms like "runway".

For example, if you're unable to get to a revenue of Rs 10L

per month by May 2023 with an ad spend of less than 30% revenue, you'll stop burning money on performance marketing and pivot your business to B2B channels of customer acquisition.

Such "turnaround times" will then become a promise to self to not fall prey to the sunk cost fallacy of pursuing something which is not worthwhile, and gives the team a tangible target, which is not "Oh shoot, our money is over and we don't have any runway left".

119. ESOPs for Employees

How many ESOPs should you give your employees? There are no rules set in stone to decide the ESOP payout, but the following framework could be used by startup founders to arrive at a workable formula.

ESOPs granted are typically a multiple of the annual CTC. The multiple could be 1x or 2x at the beginning of the start-up, to being 0.25 times the annual CTC at a later stage.

As an example, at the early stages (first two years of a company), they could offer ESOPs of a value 2x of CTC - which vests over a 4-year period. Now, assuming in the next 4 years, the company doubles in value - then the ESOP value will be 4x of one year's annual CTC spread over 4 years. That means, the employee has made 4 year's cash salary and 4 year's ESOPs salary over 4 years.

The employee is supposed to pay an exercise price, which may be equal to the face value of the share in the initial years (minimum exercise price allowed under law), but at later stages, let's say after a couple of rounds of funding have been raised, the exercise price for any new joinee may be the last fair value per share because such new employee shall only be adding value above that amount.

In terms of annual increment, one could do something like: either take a 10% hike to the in-hand salary, or a 40% hike in ESOPs' value.

All of these ideas are to be thought through in sync with various factors such as the stage of the company, valuation goals over the next few years, size of the ESOP pool, stocks available with leadership, and to whom they are being offered.

If you get a co-founder on board after two years of running the startup and maybe after one or two rounds of raise, on average, 2-7% may be the amount of equity in the company one might give away.

Remember, the above are only thinking frameworks and guidelines but not absolute truths. However, I hope they can be used as a starting point while structuring ESOPs.

120. Raise Funds or Bootstrap?

How does one decide if they should raise external funds for their startup or just bootstrap?

I believe the decision to be about balancing two out of the following three things. You will have to sacrifice one of the three, depending on what route you decide to take.

1. Scale
2. Speed
3. Freedom

If you choose scale and speed, you'd want to raise external funds for the same and you will have to sacrifice your freedom to an external investor's control on major decision-making of the business and the metrics to run after which are in the best financial interest of the investor.

If you choose to sacrifice scale, well you can build a profitable business with speed in a bootstrapped fashion, where the speed is a function of how much of your own capital and time you can invest to serve and capture a small market.

If you choose to sacrifice speed, then in a bootstrapped fashion, if you keep working, you can also scale the business across multiple years. A good example is how Physics Wallah used content to scale organically over the years.

121. Number of Investors on Cap Table

Is it okay to have 40-50 individual investors on your startup's cap table?

As a rule of thumb, you should opt for as few people on the cap table as possible, but circumstances and the stage of the startup can dictate different terms and conditions. The answer depends majorly on one factor: do you know the people on your cap table personally?

If you have raised money for your startup through a friends and family round, it is likely that you have personal relationships with these folks, which come under strain as you try and build out your startup. These people can call you anytime and would ask for updates on the startup, question you on raising the next round, when can they get an exit, etc. It also becomes distracting to be answerable to multiple individuals while you are painstakingly developing your company.

However, if it's 40-50 people invested in your startup through an angel network, then it might still be okay because you don't have personal relationships with all of them, and you will only have to manage one representative of the group through the network.

The idea here is that while capital is indeed necessary for some businesses, be cognizant of where you are raising this money from and how much interpersonal overhead this adds to your plate. No one wins if you are overloaded with unnecessary interactions when you could be investing time in building your company.

122. Investor-Startup Fit

Over a third of India's unicorns have the same business model!

Out of the ~108 unicorns in the country, over a third are online marketplaces - either B2B or B2C. Statistically speaking, the chances of you creating wealth are higher with a marketplace model rather than say, building a D2C startup.

Okay, now let's list a few marketplace startups in the country and see if there's a pattern.

- Flipkart
- Swiggy
- Urban Company
- Myntra
- InfraMarket

There's one common investor in all of them!

Accel.

VC Funds themselves have considerations such as an industry fit, a stage fit, a geography fit, etc., and this definitely seems like a fit.

For any VC fund, you can check their portfolio companies on their website to see if they will invest in you.

You would want to check if they invest in the same industry: FinTech, HealthTech, EdTech, Consumer Brands, the same geography as you, and hopefully, they've not invested in someone who is a direct competitor. Then you search for news reports for when they invested in that startup and get a sense of the stage at which they invested and the average cheque size.

You can also get data from platforms like Tracxn on how much minimum shareholding a particular investor expects. Such as a few investors take no less than a 15% stake in your startup if they give you money, and this info helps massively while negotiating.

123. Golden Factors of Business Valuation

As a fundamental principle of Finance, your business valuation is a function of two things.

1. Future expected profits
2. Growth rate

It's about maintaining a balance of these two functions. Let's see how.

› Ideal Situation: High Profits + High Growth

› Early Stage Balance: Negative Profits + Exponential Growth

› Late Stage Balance: High Profits + Slow Growth

In some cases, market share can be used as a proxy for lower profitability or deferred profitability.

While building your financial model, remember that your startup can only justify a high valuation with operating losses if you show exponential growth in your projections (and in reality, i.e. traction).

Hence, the following three levers for your business will be the driving factor of your company's valuation at all times:

1. Growth rate
2. Profit %
3. Market share

124. Inflation and Startup Runway

In an inflationary environment, a startup loses approximately 1 month of runway every year.

This means that if a startup raises money to last them 12 months, by the time they get to the 11th month, their funds may be over because of inflation, in case the rate is 8% per annum. Of course, this is a simple example to drive home the point.

But startups are not supposed to just sit with the funds raised in their bank accounts.

Here's a simple formula to avoid the trap of inflation:

- Keep enough funds to last for 3 months in your current account at most
- Keep another 3 months' funds in a debt mutual fund with 90 days maturity period
- Another 3 months' funds in debt funds with 120 days maturity, and so on

Know that debt mutual funds may give about 6-7% p.a. when FDs may give just 5%.

Why debt mutual funds? Startups registered under Startup India file a Form 2 with the Income Tax Department declaring that they shall not invest their surplus funds in equities. Hence, debt mutual funds are your best hedge against rising inflation depleting your cash reserves.

125. Negotiating ESOPs at a Startup

ESOPs are one of the most popular ways through which startups try to compensate their early employees. During the initial period of building the startup, often the company is cash-constrained and will not have positive cash flows. ESOPs become their calling card for getting good talent onboard and keeping them happy. This also ensures employees have skin in the game and are motivated towards making the startup successful. For early employees, ESOPs become a good way of building wealth, as the startup gains a foothold in the industry and increases its valuation, if the company is progressing well. Hence it is important for employees to understand the intricacies of ESOPs. The following framework of questions can be used by employees to negotiate ESOPs better.

What is the value of my ESOPs?

- How many units are being offered in total?
- What percentage of the cap table?
- What is the total market value as of date?
- What is the value as a multiple of the in-hand salary?

How will my ESOPs be given to me?

- Is it through verbal promise or email or through a grant letter? (Verbal promises change but a grant letter with a board-approved policy may be more robust.)

When do my ESOPs start vesting and at what frequency?

- Do they start vesting immediately, or after some time?
- Are they straight-line or staggered in vesting with more vesting later in the vesting period?
- What is the frequency of vesting? (monthly or quarterly or annually) And if the cliff is more than one year?

Do you have an ESOP policy?

- Is it just a verbal promise or in writing, and is this approved by the board? Seek a copy of the offer to go through it in detail, and ask a CA/Lawyer in case of a confusing clause. Always keep a copy to refer to when you later need to.

What is the price at which I get my ESOPs?

- Is it at face value or at a discount to the current valuation?
- What is the discount on the current valuation?
- How much will I have to shell out in cash while exercising?
- What will be the TDS and tax impact on exercising?

What are the Exit Clauses?

- Will I have to mandatorily exercise in a few months after my resignation?
- Is there any accelerated vesting of unvested ESOPs on liquidation/acquisition?
- Has there been any buy-back of ESOPs in the past?

These questions and their answers will ensure that you as an employee are not taken for a ride and are able to exercise your rights of ESOP ownership when you get the opportunity.

And if you are an employer, this could be a good framework to ensure that your ESOP issuance process covers the answers to these questions.

126. Acquisition: The Earn-Out Model

When your startup is acquired, the acquirer may offer to buy your business in an earn-out model.

They would say, we'll give you 40% of the total price of the business today and the remaining 60% will be earned by you over the next 2 years if you achieve a few targets. Your targets could be linked to achieving X revenues, maintaining profits above Y%, etc.

It sounds extremely reasonable from the point of view of the acquirer and of course, they're justified in saying so. But know that once an acquisition is made, in most cases, the culture of the organization changes, the decision makers change, and the environment is no longer as familiar as it was earlier to help you achieve the stipulated targets.

Plus, incentives are misaligned, where you just want to hit your revenue targets at whatever cost because you want to take home your earnout, and other areas like the brand may take a beating while you work deperately to meet targets.

So if your business is getting acquired, try and keep 25% of your payout as an earnout at most, and maximize your cash earnout today, even if it means negotiating for a lower overall consideration.

This is generic advice but holds true in most acquisition cases.

127. Force Feeding Capital to Startups

What do they feed chicken to make it fat, and why? I've heard it's soy and a lot of injections (steroids and the like).

Chicken are made to be fat through force-feeding and by artificially pumping them with hormones because they want it to grow faster than its natural pace of growth, and then sell it in the market at higher rates.

What happens when you force-feed capital into a business, giving it more than it actually needs?

It starts to "burn" money. The whole culture of the company changes to a burn mindset of burning for marketing, burning to hire, and sustainability goes for a toss.

If the culture is of burning to grow, it's very difficult for a founder to come back and think like a bootstrapped profitable businessman once you've given him funds to burn for 18 months. The fast-paced growth (or the promise thereof) is a drug!

I am not saying that the capital doesn't help with business growth. There are industries where a founder may not be able to make anything of value without heavy initial capital.

I help startups raise capital, so I make money when they raise funds, but when founders ask us to change their business model for them to appear favourable to venture capital firms, we question if their objective is to build a large business or to be known as founders who raised money and are thus "superstars".

Coming back to what happens when you force-feed capital into a business and pump it up with steroids is that you make it fat to sell it in the market at a multiple of your revenue. This could be an acquisition or an IPO.

Remember, it's not being looked at as a business to stay invested in, but to pass it on and make a quick buck. And in downturns like the funding winter of 2022-2023, the real ones are filtered from the chaff, and some phenomenal businesses are made.

Keep building, and keep going.

There's creativity in constraint. There's longevity in sustainability.

128. Setting up Home Base

A question that confounds founders is where should you incorporate your startup. Singapore, Delaware, Dubai, Estonia, or India? All these locations offer different perks and advantages.

But in order to find the perfect answer, you need to answer the following two questions:

1. Where is your Go To Market? Where will you be hiring your first set of people and testing the product on initial users?

You will definitely need an entity in this location. If a major share of your employees and initial users are based in India, it makes no sense to incorporate your entity in another continent. Setting up a base in the region where you develop your product, fine-tune your offerings, raise money, and hire your core team, offers you multiple advantages while reducing operational and logistical overheads.

2. Where is your largest market?

If you're building for the Western markets, Delaware could be the place. If South East Asia, then perhaps Singapore. For certain industries in Europe, it's Estonia. For hedge funds for the world, Cayman.

Do not just think of incorporating at a location for tax planning purposes only. Such incorporations are often difficult to execute, the Indian tax laws find a way to tax you, and administrative charges to run an offshore entity will be huge.

Plan to cross the bridge when you get to it.

129. Get Insured

When you are building a startup there are many unknowns, some of which you cannot protect yourself against and should worry about when you face them. For other situations, it is necessary to have a backup.

A Directors & Officers (D&O) Insurance is a backup that is essential for a startup. When a company gets sued, often legal suits are filed against Directors of the company, which includes Founders, and sometimes family members. The insurance covers the cost of defending such legal disputes and keeps the company and director's personal assets indemnified to a reasonable degree of insurance cover.

The importance of this insurance is further validated as investors mandate having a D&O insurance cover around Series A and onwards.

There are still a couple of things to consider:

- With rising cases of lenders taking companies to bankruptcy courts and financial frauds, the overall premiums of these policies have risen by about 20%
- Given the average costs of claims, it's best to take a policy that covers a claim of up to Rs. 3 crores at least, and can go up to approximately Rs 7-10 crores. This amount may change depending on the risk profile, industry, and amount invested in the business.

Part 5
Fundraising: Getting Money in the Bank

Being an investment banker for startups, it wouldn't be right if I don't dedicate an entire section to various aspects of fund-raising. Although this is still largely a startup subject, I like to keep the topic of VCs, valuations, pitch decks, legalities, and things specific to raising money separate.

This section is similar to the previous one on Startups, just that the subset has been reduced to topics related to fund-raising. You'll find actionable insights on things to do across your fundraising journey - before you approach investors, while talking to investors, and after you get a term sheet. Some of the chapters will help you understand how VCs think and evaluate and help you prepare accordingly. And there are a few highlighting the pitfalls founders tend to fall into during their fundraising journey.

130. First Impressions

I was watching *Mind Your Manners* on Netflix last night, and this one line really shone out.

The etiquette expert Sara Jane Ho tells her clients that when evaluating a potential partner or a date for a romantic relationship, it mostly takes people no more than 2 seconds of the first impression to make their decision.

And once a poor impression is formed, it takes 8 meetings to reverse it! 8 meetings!

And you know what; it's not just dating. I see this in investor pitches all the time.

You get a 30-minute slot with an investor after a warm connect or a series of cold emails, and within the first 5-7 minutes of observing the conversation, I can mostly tell whether the founder will get a yes or no.

So, please be prepared to answer the following questions in less than 60 seconds each if any of these are thrown at you during an investor pitch.

1. What's your target customer persona?
2. What's your moat? How are you 10x better than your competition?
3. What's your traction?
4. When can you hit your next milestone that will double your value, and what is it?

5. What is the experience of the co-founders working together? How do you know each other?
6. What is the incremental benefit your customer is getting by using your product?
7. What makes you the best-suited founder to build this?
8. If this is the only round of funding you get, can you survive without any more funding? How fast will you turn profitable and break even?
9. What is your gross margin, contribution margin and unit level economics?
10. What's that one revenue vertical in your business model that contributes the most to profitability?
11. What's your Customer Acquisition Cost, and what have you done to lower it?
12. What exit plan do you have for the investor?
13. What are the complementary skills of the co-founders/ founding team?

131. What Investors Want in a Deck

Here's what investors want to see in a startup pitch, but there's more!

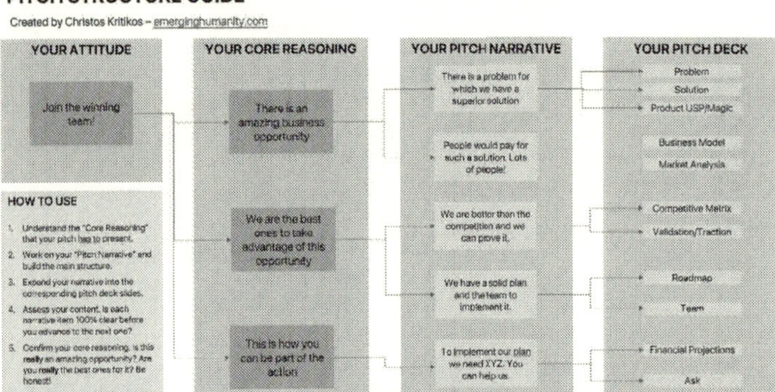

You need to explain

1. The Problem you're solving
2. How the Solution is 10x better
3. The Market size is huge
4. The Business or Revenue model
5. The Team's ability to execute

If you can't define a clear problem, you need to check if you've found Product Market Fit (PMF) or if enough people even need this.

If your solution is not 10x better (cheaper, faster, efficient) than the existing solutions, consumers may not switch to your product and you'll have massive competition from traditional as well as new players.

If the market size is not huge (say, upwards of a billion dollars annually), it may not be considered scalable or VC investable.

Your business model can be any of Subscription, eCommerce, Marketplace, SaaS, Advertising, Enterprise or Hardware. You need to know how you'll make money.

If the team's credentials don't show a spike, there may be missing examples of their skills in the field or ability to execute and scale. Solve this by forming a great founding team.

132. 5 Stories That Work

There are 5 stories that work while pitching your startup to investors!

Startup pitches are all about selling a story that's believable, inspiring, and thought-provoking, and urges an investor to say, "I want to bet on this founder and what she's building."

In this context, there are 5 stories that work. Which one do you have?

1. The Horatio Alger Story:

This is a rags-to-riches story of how the founder has been so tenacious that despite all odds, he has pushed through against all hindrances and climbed mountains to create his product or push his business. It's his sheer hard work that pushes investors to join in his journey and help him. A perfect example of this is Jugaadu Kamlesh from Shark Tank India Season 1.

2. The Charisma Story:

This story is built around an epiphany. The founder was going about her regular day when she noticed a pattern or a problem and was moved to take a step towards solving it, or realizing that it was in front of her all along and why no one else thought of this. The best example would be something like Elon Musk selling the story of electric cars through Tesla, and SpaceX and inhabiting Mars.

3. The Connections Story:

Here, the founder will drop in names such as her IIT-IIM background, her experience as a consultant at McKinsey, her work as an Executive Assistant shadowing the founder of a unicorn, or some such. I bet you know a founder who is leveraging a brand like this to build credibility and sell her or his story.

4. The Celebrity Story:

Here, the investors already know about the public persona of the founder, so it's not difficult for them to believe that this guy can sell. Think Kay Beauty with Katrina Kaif, Sonu Sood with Explurger, and my friend Raj Shamani with House of X.

5. The Experience Story:

It's the second-time founder who has built something great in the past and shown success. Kunal Shah is a great example of this.

133. Emotions Dictate Decisions

What would you do if you could feel no emotion at all?

Two guys once met with an accident and lost the part of their brains which generated emotions. Researchers thought that they would be the best subjects to study how human decisions are clouded by emotions and what would change if we removed emotions from the mix.

Both of them were given some basic facts and asked to make decisions based completely on their objective assessment of those facts.

Turned out that both the subjects had turned completely indecisive in life. No matter how clear the facts were to allow someone to make a logical decision, they were just handicapped to pick even the rational choice.

It was concluded that emotions are a necessary requirement for human decision-making and humans are incapable of decision-making if you completely eliminate emotion.

It also turned out that humans use facts and data to justify to themselves why they made a particular choice, but it's essentially a pattern in the data that makes them feel something, which helps them make a choice.

This also tells us that if you're pitching your product, service or business purely on fact, saying it's such a no-brainer, it won't help till you appeal to people's emotions.

134. 2-Minute Pitch

If you were given just 2 minutes to pitch your startup, what could you say?

I may have a framework for you.

Firstly, cover these three points in the first 30 seconds:

› What problem are you solving?

› How big is the market?

› What's your traction?

Spend the next 1.5 minutes on the following:

› What's your unique insight?

› How you make money?

› Who is in the team?

› What's the big ask?

2 minutes. 7 things in total. Cut the repetition. Close.

If it's just 30 seconds, address the first 3 points and try to include traction data if you have.

135. How to Get Investors to Open Your Email

Here's a trick to get investors to open your email.

Adding your recipient's name in the subject line increases their chances of opening the email by up to 23%, and click-through rates go up by upto 32%. Further, the unsubscribed rate reduces by upto 17%.

Researchers found this by experimenting with emails of the following three organizations:

- 11+ Lakh emails of Mercadolibre - the largest online marketplace in Latin America
- 5,000 emails of Stanford University's monthly newsletter about executive courses
- 68k+ emails of a financial analysis course selling company

While this works well for proposed customers when you send them discount codes and newsletters, I have reason to believe that this would work with investors as well when you're sending them pitch decks. It's something we almost always try to do while sending pitches of clients to Investors.

136. Get Investors to Contact You

How do you get investors to contact you, and offer to invest funds in your startup?

I have personally seen a few of our clients actually being wooed by venture investors, a couple of them competing to invest in their startups. While such situations are far and few, know that even investors are in the business of finding good deals to invest in - and they're not sitting there to say no to startups.

So, here are a few tips to making it easy for them to find you, and be interested in what you're building... because inbound leads have a much better chance of converting into a term sheet than you doing a cold outreach...

- You can list on AngelList (now, Wellfound) for recruiting talent for your startup so that you're listed and visible on a platform where investors are active.
- Get some PR activity done to have news websites, magazines or newsletters write about your novel idea, team, founders or product.
- The founder needs to build a personal brand on Linkedin/ Twitter and engage in "building in public" or "thought leadership" to shine out and be spottable.
- If you can't rightfully find the time to do this, at least make that a task that someone from the marketing team

must carry out. No shame, there are agencies who help you plan and execute this.

- Get Tracxn, Crunchbase, Pitchbook to pick you up and list your company on their platform. You can seek the help of a VC analyst friend to get the listing or just do some (noteworthy and praiseworthy) PR to be listed organically.
- Make an abridged pitch deck for your business and pin it on the top of your Linkedin profile.

If you do the above, and what you're building is exciting, you can get inbound requests to understand what you're building.

Now comes the next problem - you don't need to open up about your entire business in any such call requests.

Do a reference check on the person you're getting on a call with. A lot of VCs may also be doing these calls to understand market and competitor data for one of their existing portfolio companies or just to build a thesis document.

So, it may be worth it to get on the call, but be cautious with what information is worth disclosing and what isn't.

Also, if you're looking for plain vanilla debt funding, do nothing. You'll probably get a call from Bajaj Finance.

137. Following Up on Cold Emails

What should you do if the investor you write an email to for pitching your startup does not respond?

If you've been in this situation, you've probably thought they're not interested and decided to find the next investor on the list to write to. However, understand that if you've written a cold email, there's a high chance a busy person who receives at least 10 new cold emails daily, would not respond to you.

It makes sense to give them about 3-4 days and write back a polite email asking if they found time to see your email and seek confirmation if it fits their investment thesis.

It would help to mention that you studied their portfolio and thought it's a good fit because of a few key highlights of your product or business. Showcase the best traits of your product, market, and team!

The chances of people responding to cold emails increase even if you follow up just once!

So, remember that the best trait of a founder is their tenacity, so be politely tenacious, and follow up.

138. Due Diligence by Investors

The following 8 form part of the basic legal agreements and drafts, which are checked at the time of Due Diligence for all startups when they approach investors for raising funds.

1. Co-Founders Agreement: The co-founders need to agree on the following items in writing:
   - Capital contribution
   - Time, effort and deliverables
   - Decision making, voting rights and veto powers
   - Vesting / Reverse vesting of Equity
   - Restrictions on share transfer
2. Shareholders Agreement: If you've taken funds from friends & family or angels or any kind of investor, there would be a Shareholders Agreement (SHA), which is incorporated also within the Articles of Association of the company. This defines the rights and responsibilities of all shareholders including founders and others. It is different from a Share Subscription Agreement (SSA), or at times combined with it to form an SSHA.
3. NDA: Keep a simple yet robust Non-Disclosure Agreement (NDA) draft ready to be executed with all employees and early developers, contractors, vendors, etc. Get it

signed while onboarding people.

4. Employment Letter: There is typically an offer letter and once the offer letter is accepted by the employee, an employment letter is issued which also has clauses on vesting, intellectual property, confidentiality, KPIs, compensation, variable pay, ESOPs, etc. A detailed ESOP Policy and Grant Letter are actually made separately.

5. Vendor Agreement: There are 3 types of vendor agreements - one for the purchase of goods, another for services, and a third for contractual staff not on your payroll.

6. SaaS Agreement: When you click "accept" on any online terms & conditions or click-wrap agreements while signing up for subscriptions of software services, etc - do you maintain copies of what you've signed/agreed to for reference later? If not, know that such terms are later very difficult to extract, and you should ideally keep them all in print pdf form from the moment you accept them.

7. Terms & Conditions: These are certain terms and conditions that your users/customers/consumers agree to when visiting and engaging with your website. This should indemnify you if someone meets a loss while engaging with your site.

8. Privacy Policy: This policy seeks to take approval or consent from users on how their personal data will be used and analyzed at the back end by the company.

139. Equity Dilution with Each Round

How much equity should you dilute in your startup at each stage of funding?

In 2019, a research firm analyzed data from 8000 startups from Crunchbase to pull out the following insights.

› Angel and seed round dilutions are mostly between 10-15%

› The median percent of shares acquired by investors peaks at Series A and then trends down as company valuations increase - this is mostly an average of 20%

But why? Prior to Series A, angel and seed investors typically invest smaller amounts of money when the risk of failure is very high but the potential reward is also massive, so they don't require stakes as large as institutional investors.

For institutional investors that come in at Series A, they know they need a stake of a minimum of 15% to make their projected returns on the entire portfolio of startup investments to give an exit to their investors.

Later-stage rounds tend to minimise dilution because with lower risks and higher valuations, VCs know they can make large enough returns even with single-digit stakes.

It is also believed that Series A funding is the hardest to secure because failure rates spike between Seed and Series A. So VCs have a high bargaining power at this point.

140. Raising Venture Debt

How to know if you are eligible to raise Venture Debt funding? Usually, you should meet the following criteria:

- You should have raised at least a Series A round already, i.e. minimum ~Rs 20 crores.
- You should have at least a 15-month runway left with that money.
- The Venture Debt investment may be up to 15-20% of the amount of your last equity fundraise.
- You should have revenues for a product that has positive unit economics.

Venture Debt helps fund working capital requirements without diluting equity in your startup. Plus, there's not much of due diligence or valuation required as all of that was done in the recent past during Series A.

The cost of debt is upwards of 17% p.a. Venture Debt firms also take a warrant in your startup which is a small right to hold some shareholding in your company if the valuation continues to rise.

Some of the top Venture Debt funds in India include Alteria Capital, Innoven Capital, Stride Ventures, and Trifecta Capital.

141. Right Questions

The biggest mistake people make while ending a presentation is saying, "Happy to take any questions."

The mistake is even bigger if such a question comes at the end of a sales presentation. For startup founders when they're pitching to investors, it's a presentation to sell their equity!

The reason it's not the right approach is that if the investor (buyer) is not interested, they don't give you any feedback to address their concerns and make the sale. Founders may get run-of-the-mill answers like, "You're too early for us", or "We're no longer looking at this market."

The right questions to ask at the end of the pitch are:

1. Would you want to invest in such a business?
2. If they say no, ask them what metrics would you want to see for this to be an investible business.
3. If that gets them talking about the MRR, DAU, GMV, etc., ask if you could achieve that in x months, would they agree to invest in you?

This is just one way to get them to give relevant information. You could build another line of questioning to extract more information.

It's not the job of the prospective buyer to ask questions, but that of the salesperson! That's what the founder here is.

142. What VC Funds Want

There are three things that every VC Fund wants to see in a startup.

1. Past Achievements of the Founders / Founding Team

VCs back a killer team even before they look at the product or the market. If there was just one deciding factor, it would be the Founding Team. Therefore, it helps if you're an IIT-IIM guy or one from a marquee academic institute. It helps if you have worked in Management Consulting in McKinsey or BCG.

If none of that, it helps if you've achieved something which could be national news, or at least state level. Or if you've built something great as a part of an organisation in your employment. Past achievements of founders matter.

Think, it's the same as showing a spike on your MBA application or on your resume. Past achievements that differentiate you and show that you can hustle and execute better than others matter. This is especially important if you're trying to raise money at the early stage and have little in terms of traction or product.

2. Serving an Unmet Need in a Growing Market

65% of startups die because they're building a product that not enough people want.

It's not the best product that wins, it's the product that can sell the most, which does. Or, the founder, who can sell it the best, who does. This is why the size of the market and its growth rate is more important than the product

3. A 10x Product

Your Product must be 10x better than the existing solution - 10x faster, 10x cheaper, or 10x more efficient. Thus, it always helps that you have a Minimum Viable Product and traction numbers to show before you approach a VC for funding - or customer validation, Net Promoter Scores, etc

Remember, it's in that preferential order: Founder, Market Size, Product (Traction)

143. VC Method of Valuation

Most Founders have NO IDEA about this method by which VCs value their startups!

The VC Method of valuation was developed in 1987 by a Harvard Business School Professor.

In this case, the VC first estimates an exit valuation and then works backward to think how can they make a 20X return on exit by fixing a value to the business today. Let's look at it through a simple example.

Target Exit Valuation = 100 Crore

Return wanted on Exit = 20x

Thus, ideal post money valuation today = 100/20 = 5 Crore

Amount being invested in the startup = 1 Crore

Pre-Money Valuation = 5-1 = 4 Crores

Now, let's assume the investor's shares will be diluted by 50% in future rounds. So pre-money value of the startup adjusted for future dilution = 4/2 = 2 Crores

The next natural question that comes up is how they determine the target exit value of the business after 8 years.

They do this by estimating, say, in the 8th year from now, the company will have revenues of 80 Crores, on which say the profit will be 10% at 8 Crores. In the 8th year, it is expected the PE Multiple for companies in the same sector to be 15. This means the company's value will be 15 times its profit. Then 15 x 8 = 120 Crores, which is the target exit valuation.

I recommend startups use multiple methods before going ahead and pitching to an investor so that their valuation ask is validated through all possible valuation models.

144. Pledge funds vs VC Funds

Do you know what are Pledge Funds and how they differ from Venture Capital Funds for startup investing?

VC Firms raise a fixed amount of capital (fund amount) from their investors (Limited Partners) and then decide which startups to invest the money in. The investment decision for each startup including cheque size and mechanics of the deal is decided by the Investment Committee run by the General Partner (GP).

However, a Pledge Fund is like a syndicate of investors who don't pool all their money into an existing fund but decide to invest in each deal or startup on a deal-by-deal basis. A few investors from the fund may like a particular deal and may commit a certain amount to it, but a few others may choose not to invest.

In Pledge Funds, investors have more individual say in which startups they want to back, whereas, in VC Funds, the GP takes those decisions independently of the LPs.

People also call the Pledge Fund model as Capital on Call Model, and most Angel Syndicates in India are structured in this form.

145. What to Do After Getting a Term Sheet

Three things to do after getting an investor term sheet.

1. Get a Second Term Sheet

Having an alternate gives you bargaining power. So ensure that if you're talking to multiple investors who could be leads, line them up in a way that at least two of them offer the term sheet at the same time. Negotiation is all about BATNA(Best Alternative To a Negotiated Agreement), and you create it with a comparative alternate.

2. Investor Due Diligence

Speak with at least two founders who were backed by this investor and their startups shit down, so that you understand what this investor is like to work with when things go south.

3. Negotiate the Terms

Don't just sign it out of excitement. You need to understand all terms with a professional and then negotiate them well before you agree.

146. For D2C Brands Raising Funds

If you run a D2C brand, here are 4 points of reality check before you go out to raise funds.

1. Revenue Numbers

There are hundreds of brands right now doing more than Rs 1 crore per month in sales and bootstrapped, which are out there to raise their first round of funding so don't be surprised if investors think your annual revenue run rate of Rs 3 crores is not enough traction. There are so many founders who watch Shark Tank and think 25 lakhs of monthly sales are phenomenal and they deserve an award because they heard Sharks say "wow" when a founder mentioned that figure on the TV show.

2. Valuation

Revenue Multiples for valuation are down to 2.5x to 4x (at best). Thinking someone will give you a 5-6x revenue multiple or more is the exception and not the norm!

3. Profits

Investors now seemingly want EBITDA-positive D2C brands to invest in, who will use the funds for boosting growth in capex and geographical expansion and not for working capital. Debt is cheaper for working capital, not equity, certainly not VC money.

4. Distribution

Performance Marketing is darn expensive, and the focus has to be on offline expansion. The real moat now lies in cracking offline distribution through wholesaler and distributor networks to get their product in not just modern trade but even kirana stores

P.S. Please do not learn about valuation multiples and the definition of kickass traction or "wow" from 10-minute segments you see on Shark Tank. You need to show a legit business that makes everyone money.

147. Difference Between ROFR and ROFO

ROFR (Right of First Refusal) and ROFO (Right of First Offer) are important terms of an investor term sheet.

ROFR means that if any shareholder in the company (say, founders) wishes to sell some of their shares to a third party, they will first have to offer those shares for purchase to the existing investor who has ROFR rights. The founder cannot sell to any other person without offering the shares to the investor. They can sell to third parties only if the investor refuses to buy at the same rate or more.

ROFO on the other hand means Right of First Offer, which means before you talk to anyone else about selling your shares, you must offer the shares to the person holding ROFO rights, so that he can offer a price at which he could purchase the shares.

Investors may prefer to have a ROFR when they feel they would want a selling shareholder to do the hard work of finding the best value for their shares in the open market, and then come back to them to ask them to match the best rate, if any such rate is offered, and it makes sense for the investor.

Investors typically have visibility on the true value of a company due to access to information on the business, and if they refuse to buy the shares (despite having the monetary ability to buy), the third-party buyer may feel that he has offered too much and may reduce his price or not go ahead. Thus, it can work against founders in this case.

ROFR helps investors find and match the best price in the market to buy more stakes in the company.

Negotiating against ROFR, founders typically seek ROFO rights for themselves, saying that in case the investors want to sell their shares, they must make the first offer to sell to the founders, so that founders can get a heads up on the investor wanting to exit, and they can find a way to fund the purchase of such shares and keep shareholding in their closed circle of trusted confidantes.

Must remember though that the situations where either may be beneficial vary from case to case and the objective of the shareholder with respect to the duration of holding such investment.

148. Don't Fall Into This VC Trap

A lot of marquee VC firms which would invest from Series A and onwards started setting up funds to invest small ticket sizes at the Seed stage as well, in the last few years. You may have seen 5L cheques from some such global funds in startups.

A founder would think that it's great because once you have a big VC on your cap table, other investors will easily pitch in that round.

However, if you think from the VC's perspective, instead of writing one cheque of 1 Cr into a startup, they've written cheques of 5L in 20 competing startups and diversified their risk. Now, the VC gets access to your monthly financial and operating data as part of the MIS report, something they would otherwise never get access to, even with Tracxn or Crunchbase subscriptions. The VC will probably back just a couple of those competitors in the next round at Series A and choose to not back the remaining.

In Series A, if the same fund decides to not back you, no other marquee VC will fund you as they'll know that there may be something wrong in the startup that the other VC chose to not fund the next round.

Not that every VC at the early stage does this, but it's always good for a founder to know that such practices exist.

149. Size of ESOP Pool During Fundraise

How to determine the size of your ESOP Pool at the time of each fundraise?

At the time of your first raise from a VC, they may require you to mandatorily create an unissued ESOP pool of 10% pre-money, which in most cases, you may have to agree to in the guise of this being a standard clause. There are arguments against this too, but let's keep that aside for the time being and assume we agree to 10%.

At the time of all subsequent fundraises, you should ideally have the unissued part of the pool at half of the issued part of the ESOP pool, assuming you're doing rounds every 18-24 months.

For example, if you've issued 8% from the first pool, then you need to maintain about 4% unissued. So, you may want to stretch your ESOP pool from 10% to 12%, so that you have 8% issued and 4% unissued, which will be used to issue more ESOPs to new hires, etc.

The unissued portion should be 50% at each step because with each new raise, the value of your ESOPs increases, and you can hire more people by issuing fewer ESOPs.

This is not an absolute method, but one way of logically thinking through the size rather than just setting 20% aside and diluting the founder equity with no mathematical basis.

150. Where Does VC Money Go?

Where is the majority of all Venture Capital money going? Here's attempting an answer.

If you look at the financials or the use of funds of startups, at least 30-40% of it is allocated to customer acquisition and marketing spends.

As per a Matrix Partners India report, the CAC per user increased by 1.7 times in just 10 months from 2021 to 2022. That's because all companies are competing to bid a higher amount to target similar customers across segments.

Now, who are the beneficiaries of a majority of this advertising and marketing spend?

Google, Facebook, Amazon!

So as a prudent investor, where should you be putting your money? Especially at a time when these tech stocks are much below their highs (as of May 2023).

Not to say that you shouldn't invest in startups, but evaluate them basis efficiencies in CAC or marketing spends to achieve their north star metrics.

Startups that work on building tighter-knit communities and cohorts, and then attempt to add value to serve the needs of such communities with their products or services are able to achieve PMF at a much lower CAC in the early stages.

151. Fund Your D2C Startup Without Diluting

If you wish to start a D2C brand in say, beverages, snacks, fashion, personal care, etc - then instead of raising funds from VCs where you dilute equity in your company, you could go for Revenue Based Financing (RBF).

These firms give you funds that you can use for marketing to drive more sales, and then repay the amount as a percentage of the total sales revenue on a monthly basis.

This helps you maintain full control over your business and get funds without any security or collateral.

The amount that they offer as funding depends on your past few months' sales and your gross margin. They shall audit that data, and determine the best amount for you.

List of RBF investors are:

› Klub

› GetVantage

› Velocity

› Recur

› N+1 Capital

152. Subjective Valuation of Startups

Valuation is a tricky game. Moreover, there is no right or wrong approach to what is inherently a very subjective idea. Let's understand the different lenses different types of investors utilize while valuing the same business.

Angel Investors

- They expect to make a 2-5X return on their investment in 4-5 years
- You are able to sell the idea to VCs over the next 2-3 rounds
- Get them an exit through of sale of their shares to the VC at Series A/B
- They primarily back the Founder and how novel/feasible their idea is
- Usually, there are no revenues or EBITDA multiples to base the valuation on, and hence there is no method to the valuation
- Negotiations revolve around the minimum ticket size of equity that will satisfy them

Venture Capital Firms

- They will evaluate the Founders' credentials and ability to execute, the market size for the product, and the moat

- They hope to get a return of 15-20X on their Investment in the next 5 years - stretched to a maximum of 8 years
- Usually reinvest in the immediate next round(s) if you're doing well
- Will use Revenue Multiples of competitors (adjusted to their conviction) at the growth stage
- They do not use DCF or the EBITDA Multiple methods of valuation
- They have a rough calculation of the average cheque size and the minimum equity they take in all deals
- They will mostly fund the next 18-24 months of your runway for 15-20% of your company's stake

Private Equity Investors

- Hope you can get them a 2-4X Return on their investment in the next 2-3 years at IPO
- They use EBITDA multiples and try to extrapolate your value based on PE multiples of listed competitors
- They require you to scale revenue and Profits to get a minimum 2-4X at IPO
- Use the DCF method and at times will place a CFO in your Management to help get you to IPO at a target value

Strategic Investor

- They are interested in obtaining a majority stake or 100% buyout to eat the small fish as a big fish

- They can afford to buy what you've built with their surplus cash rather than build it from scratch themselves
- They target to give you a Revenue Multiple or PE Multiple less than their own
- At times can overpay by a huge margin as they could hugely overestimate the benefit they will get from your product (story of most M&A deals)
- They can be ego-driven to acquire you to either kill competition in the market or to stay relevant with the latest product/offering
- Their investments are usually driven by the idea of a horizontal or vertical integration into their own core business

The above pointers can be debated in that they are too simplistic and not every investor follows the same principle, but at the core of it, valuation is a function of future profit potential, and an expected growth rate. Both are driven by the story that you as a Founder can sell. Also, there's never one answer to a valuation. There could be a range and in fact even multiple bands of ranges for each type of investor. Because "value" at the end of the day is based on the buyer's motivation and willingness to pay.

153. VC's Lawyer Fees

As you progress on your journey of building a startup, you will face quite a few absurdities. One of them comes about when you have a VC onboard who is interested in investing capital in your startup.

Most marquee VCs, when they come on board, a "standard" term on the term sheet requires the startup to bear the legal fees for the VC's lawyer as well. It is akin to paying the VC's lawyer out of your own pocket while the lawyer is trying to negotiate against you in favor of the VC.

However, unfortunately for startups, this clause has become standard in the industry, and you as a founder may have to pay the fees. The explanation behind this happening is that the VCs will have to bear these fees from their management fees if they were to bear the cost themselves, and passing it on to the startup helps them offload it.

As I mentioned this has become a norm and if you're in a place where you feel you can't get away without bearing the cost, then the best course of action is to implement a damage control mechanism. Try and negotiate a cap on the legal fees to be paid, so that the lawyer is not unnecessarily negotiating just to bill more hours.

Book Recommendations

How much water do you add to flour to make the perfect dough?

While I'm not gifted at cooking, I can get by when left to fend for myself in the kitchen, which includes having to make dough sometimes. It's a game of trial and error for me, but my mum can do it with much lesser thought and effort.

Now you're probably good at making dough that'll last your family a day, but what if you had to estimate quantities for making dough for 500 people?

I recently read that the ideal ratio for bread dough is 5 parts flour to 3 parts water. And this has been a game-changer. Most people who can very intuitively make sense of how to knead dough, would probably not know of this exact thumb rule.

And this is exactly what happens in business. You're probably okay at running a bootstrapped business profitably and managing a 20-member team. But what happens when the teams have to be increased to 200, and revenues to be increased by 100 times?

If intuition and common sense make small businesses profitable, it's frameworks that help them scale.

And I thought I'll take this opportunity to list a few of my favorite books if you want to learn about frameworks for scaling up your business.

1. *Good to Great: Why Some Companies Make the Leap and Others Don't* by Jim Collins
2. *Great by Choice: Uncertainty, Chaos, and Luck—Why Some Thrive Despite Them All* by Jim Collins
3. *Blue Ocean Strategy* by W. Chan Kim
4. *Untangling Conflict: An Introspective Guide for Families in Business* by Janmejaya Sinha
5. *Working Backwards: Insights, Stories, and Secrets from Inside Amazon* by Colin Bryar
6. *Contagious: Why Things Catch On* by Jonah Berger
7. *The Embedded Entrepreneur: How to Build an Audience-Driven Business* by Arvid Kahl
8. *Influence: The Psychology of Persuasion* by Robert Cialdini
9. *The Cold Start Problem: How to Start and Scale Network Effects* by Andrew Chen
10. *Confessions of the Pricing Man* by Hermann Simon
11. *Extreme Revenue Growth* by Victor Cheng
12. *Attention Factory: The Story of TikTok and China's ByteDance* by Matthew Brennan
13. *Daily Coffee & Startup Fundraising* by Sarthak Ahuja (subtle plugin)

14. *The Basics of Bitcoins and Blockchains* by Antony Lewis
15. *The Psychology of Money* by Morgan Housel
16. *Venture Deals* by Brad Feld
17. *Never Split the Difference: Negotiating As If Your Life Depended On It* by Chris Voss
18. *The CEO Factory: Management Lessons from Hindustan Unilever* by Sudhir Sitapati
19. *The Firm: The Inside Story of McKinsey* by Duff McDonald
20. *How Will You Measure Your Life* by Clayton Christensen

Acknowledgements

Almost none of the thoughts in this book are my own. I read books and blogs and often give a spin to some of those theories to suit the context I work in. It is a compilation of my learnings coupled with my experience of using these concepts in my work as an investment banker and advisor to startups and family businesses. Everything I've written in this book is my interpretation of what other experts and thought leaders have painstakingly concluded.

This book is a result of my habit of documenting the learnings and insights I come across on a daily basis. None of that would be possible without my perpetual partner in crime and wife, Aditi Randev. I need to thank her for all my branding, online and offline persona. She has brought structure and sanity to my life which enables me to create the work I do. This book, ultimately, is as much her effort as mine. Also I want to thank my parents right next to God for their blessings and sacrifices in raising me right.

Thanks to the folks at Wyzr - Yashraj and Amlan, and my dear friend Vinit Aggarwal for agreeing to take up this project. Publishing 2 books by the same author in a span of 8 months is unheard of, but these guys have such an effective process in place that speed is never a problem. Given their extensive knowledge of business, I know I can always rely on them with the final output. This book would not have been possible without them.

Finally, thanks to my ever-curious audience on social media for constantly pushing me to learn more, and to you, the reader, for showing faith in me by picking this book up.

About the Author

Sarthak Ahuja has over a decade of experience in startup advisory. He is a Chartered Accountant and a Gold Medalist from the Indian School of Business.

As an investment banker, he's worked with companies in SaaS, e-Commerce, and D2C, in industries such as FinTech, EdTech, Gaming, Healthcare, and F&B, among others. He's also an Executive Coach and a faculty of M&A at top-tier business schools in India.

He creates educational content for the founder community on his social media platforms with a combined following of over 400K as of June 2023.

He is also the author of *Daily Coffee & Startup Fundraising*, a detailed guide on starting up and raising funds in India and the Middle East.

You can follow him on LinkedIn and on his Instagram handle @casarthakahuja.

Made in the USA
Middletown, DE
17 June 2025

77161448R00168